"The story has multiple murder tential culprits, and possibly n twists and turns. One moment pears clear, and the next the sa script is engaging, entertaining, highly credible, and well worth your time. ... The play's author, Richard Weill, is both a trial attorney and an experienced playwright. Consequently, the script bears an uncommon authenticity, as well as being literate, concise and cogent. His characters offer valuable insights on the differences between being 'innocent' and 'not guilty,' plus richly balanced observations about the impact of the media on the justice system."

> — Jim Spencer and Shirley Lorraine (Two on the Aisle: "Intrigue abounds in *Framed* at the Elite"), *Ventura Breeze*, May 11, 2016

"Weill's courtroom experience is evident in both the attorneys' background discussions and in the snippets of trial scenes in a play that opens with a dead body — and it's not the last of them."

> — Rita Moran ("Whodunit '*Framed*' will keep audience guessing"), *Ventura County Star*, May 13, 2016

"Ingenious."

> — Elissa Durwood, former critic, *London Times Literary Supplement*

"*Framed* was a hit. *Framed* was entertaining, intriguing and made audiences think about the process and culture of our legal system. No play on our South Stage has received the standing-room-only audience numbers that Framed delivered. ... Thank you for honoring Elite Theatre Company with the World Premiere of *Framed*."

> — Tom Eubanks, Artistic Director, Elite Theatre Company, Oxnard, California

WE OPEN IN OXNARD
SATURDAY AFTERNOON

FRAMED

We Open in Oxnard Saturday Afternoon

Framed

Richard Weill

Sidney Books
NEW YORK

www.sidneybooks.com

Interior typeface: Book Antiqua
Cover typeface: Marker Felt

Photo credit (Back Cover): Shoshana Hantman

ISBN: 978-0-9913512-9-9

First Sidney Books trade paperback edition May 2018

10 9 8 7 6 5 4 3 2 1

To Anthony Shaffer, Ira Levin, Frederick Knott,
A.A. Milne, Patrick Hamilton, Dame Agatha,
and all other practitioners of this
"trickiest and most demanding of genres" —

to Tom, Judy, Vivien, Alexander, Larry, Olivia,
Ken, Nancy, Johnny, Jake, Chris, Bethany,
and everyone else at the Elite Theatre Company —

and, above all, to Shoshana

"Take it home, boys. We open in Leavenworth Saturday night."

— Mel Brooks, *The Producers*

CONTENTS

The Elite Theatre Company occupies a light gray clapboard building in a shopping area on South Victoria Avenue in Oxnard, California. The two-story theater building faces a marina and, in a way, resembles an upscale beach house. Inside are two theaters on opposite sides of a spacious lobby: the Main Stage, with its auditorium seating, wide stage, and extensive lighting and sound controls; and the South Stage, a smaller venue with rows of chairs, a confined stage, and limited technical options.

Only black curtains separate each stage from the lobby. This means the Elite can't present shows in both theaters simultaneously. So its weekend schedule is staggered. On Friday and Saturday nights and Sunday afternoons, the Main Stage is open. South Stage plays—including the Elite's World Premiere productions—are performed on Saturday afternoons and Sunday evenings.

For this reason, the Elite's World Premiere production of my first produced play — a legal thriller entitled *Framed* — opened, not at night, but on a Saturday afternoon: May 7, 2016. According to Google Maps, the opening was 2,841 miles from my home in Westchester County, New York. Also according to Google Maps, driving these 2,841 miles would take 40 hours (with no traffic).

The trip to Oxnard had taken me 40 years.

I wrote my first play in the summer of 1976, the summer between my graduating college and beginning law school. Actually, I wrote two plays that summer: a political comedy and a one-man biography (much in vogue at the time). And I wrote two plays the next summer: a drama based on my grandfather's memoirs as a young artist and a thinly disguised (i.e., *Inherit the Wind*-style) account of the 1919 Black Sox scandal (before everyone started retelling that story).

Nothing came of these plays, or the ones that followed: a play set in the New York Civil Jail and a musical version of *Waiting for Godot*.

So in the early 1990's I took a cold, hard look at what I was writing and concluded that I had few insights into the plight of mankind or the human condition. I had been raised in a normal, happy home. I had faced no severe deprivations. I had become a successful prosecutor in suburban New York with a loving wife and, in time, two young children. My sufferings were not the result of any follies but my own.

I had two talents as a playwright: I could write funny, and I could write clever. And that's when I decided to write the next great American stage thriller.

Stage thrillers had always fascinated me, ever since I saw the original production of *Deathtrap* shortly after its opening in 1978. It was a fascination I shared with my father (who remembered thrillers from the early 1930's like *Riddle Me This* and *Whistling in the Dark*, and often would recount the latter's plot twist involving poison inserted in a toothpaste tube).

No genre places a premium on originality like the stage thriller. Your plot twist(s) cannot reuse what other have used before. Accordingly, I had to immerse myself in every stage thriller script I could find, and every book or article on the genre, to catalogue ideas I couldn't use because someone else got there first.

I also learned the clichés of the genre: mystery-writer protagonists; triangle plays featuring a husband, wife, and lover, with two of the three conspiring against the third (and the audience uncertain throughout which two are the true conspirators).

My first opportunity to write a thriller came when my wife and I took an evening class for playwrights and actors at a local performing arts college. The premise of the class was that playwrights benefitted from hearing actors read their work, and actors' audition skills benefitted from performing freshly written scenes. My wife joined the actors' section; I joined the playwrights.

I had 60% of a good idea for a thriller that I called *Imperfect Alibi*: a wife needs irrefutable proof that her husband is having an affair, so she fakes her own murder and frames her husband for the apparent crime, forcing him to prove the affair to the investigating police detective as his alibi. When the wife reappears and reveals her scheme, the husband realizes that his rock-solid alibi lets him kill her *now*, as long as he does so in the manner she foretold, and the body remains undiscovered long enough to prevent determining a precise time of death. That was Act I.

Act II begins with the arrival of a different police detective than the one to whom the husband proved his alibi — because no such first policeman exists. He had proven his alibi to an imposter hired by his wife. That was Act II, Scene 1.

The rest of Act II remained a mystery (that I didn't solve for twenty years, when I realized that two incomplete ideas of mine could be combined to make one complete play).

The first thriller I completed was a two-character play, *Seed of Doubt*. It was based on an actual murder case: a husband and wife were proceeding through an amicable divorce until the wife met a divorce lawyer at a party, began an affair with the lawyer, the lawyer intervened in the divorce and bilked the husband of everything — whereupon the husband murdered the lawyer. In my play, the murder already has occurred. A police detective is responding to the husband's house to investigate. The play is a cat-and-mouse game between the two — some real, some imagined.

I wrote it because the Mystery Writers of America announced that its October 1998 Boucheron convention in Philadelphia would feature a mystery play competition, with the winning play to be performed at the Society Hill Playhouse. Prior to the submission deadline, a close friend of my wife, active in her local theater in upstate New York, offered to arrange a reading of my play by two actors in her company. The reading was done at a table, without rehearsal. The experience was somewhat deflating.

On the ride home, I told my wife of another idea I had, entitled *The Other Woman*. Its premise was that a husband and his "wife" rent a remote cottage, claiming to be on the run from another woman who has threatened them. Soon we learn that the "wife" is really the husband's lover in disguise, and that their plan is, first, to establish her as his wife with the local community, and then to lure the real wife to the cottage, murder her apparently in self-defense, and identify her as the threatening "other woman." And the twists keep coming from that point on. It was a classic triangle play.

My wife loved the idea. I wrote the play fairly quickly and submitted both *Seed of Doubt* and *The Other Woman* to the Boucheron competition.

Neither won.

Additional ideas followed. One was a two-character play about early 20th century detective-story writer Jacques Futrelle, who wrote one of the great "impossible escape" tales ever ("The Problem of Cell 13"), yet in real life went down with the RMS Titanic. The premise of the play (*Problem at Sea*), to be performed on a bare stage representing the Titanic's deck, was that Futrelle and his fictional detective, Professor Van Dusen, would apply their collective wisdom to finding an escape from the sinking ship. But I could never figure out how to structure a full-length play from the idea (so years later, at long last, wrote it as a one-act play).

Another was an idea about a person with multiple personalities that came to me while reading a copy of John Pielmeier's Edgar-award-winning thriller *Voices in the Dark*, also about multiple personality disorder. Halfway through the play, I was 100% certain I knew what the play's big twist would be. I was wrong — but I liked my twist so much that I was determined to use it myself. But, again, turning it into a full-length play eluded me (so again this finally became a one-act play, *Mistaken Identity*).

And then there was the comment someone made about the standard array of stock supporting characters in most Agatha Christie novels. Suddenly, I imagined the cast of a repertory company performing mystery novel after mystery novel, exchanging roles occasionally, but never knowing anything about their characters beyond the words on the page. It was to be entitled *Stilettos at Teatime* – ultimately the one-act play *Perhaps She'll Die*.

There were many false starts between 1998 and 2008, but nothing new completed. Some resulted in a few notes on a memo pad. Others simply became a title on a running list I maintained on my computer. One I actually outlined from beginning to end, but was never satisfied enough to proceed further.

I discovered that beneath a seemingly great thriller idea were often seemingly insurmountable plot flaws. Unfortunately, whatever notes I kept never referenced these flaws. As a result, I'd bounce back to an old idea with a rush of renewed enthusiasm, only to have to discover the flaws all over again.

Furthermore, I was starting to question the current viability of the stage thriller. Broadway wasn't producing them any more. They weren't taken seriously. And yet, they remained a staple in local theaters around the county, because audiences still loved them. Most new productions were revivals. Occasionally a new thriller would surface in a regional theater somewhere. But the occasions were infrequent.

Then in August 2008, I was surfing the Internet and happened upon the website for the International Mystery Writers' Festival in Owensboro, Kentucky. And that's how *Framed* began its road to the stage that ended almost eight years later in Oxnard, California.

Upon first reading about the International Mystery Writers' Festival, I was struck by one thought: why didn't I know about this before? I had tried my best to keep up with the stage thriller world, searching periodically for news about new plays. But the Festival already had completed two annual events, in June 2007 and June 2008, while escaping my notice.

The Festival was the brainchild of producer Zev Buffman (who later won the Mystery Writers of America's coveted Raven Award for this achievement). Its sole purpose was to revive and perpetuate the stage thriller as a discrete theatrical form. From submitted plays, ten finalists were chosen, produced, and performed during the two-week Festival, along with other events. Then prizes — Angies — were awarded. In fact, all three nominees for the "best play" Edgar in 2008 had premiered at the Festival in 2007.

However, there would be no 2009 edition. The Festival was taking a year off. According to its website, it would next be held in June 2010, with an August 2009 submission deadline. In other words, I had exactly one year to complete the best thriller ever written.

At first, I considered resubmitting *The Other Woman*. It had an extremely clever plot, and a lot of sharp, biting humor. I had revised it substantially since its prior submission, adding themes and dimensions missing from the original version. One such addition was inspired by an interview I'd once watched with actress Lili Palmer, in which she said that the worst form of adultery was not sexual infidelity, but the betrayal of marital secrets. The loss of trust became the spine of the play.

But for all of its pluses, *The Other Woman* had one key drawback: at its heart, it was a triangle play, a thriller cliché. No, my submission had to be something fresh and exciting.

[*WARNING: It is impossible to tell the story of* Framed, *both its writing (including a dozen rewrites) and its production, without spoiling its plot twists. Those who wish to experience* Framed *on paper unspoiled should stop here, turn to page 73, and return here after reading the play.*]

I thought of great thrillers that are a pastiche of an already well-established mystery genre. *Sleuth* evokes the recognizable characteristics of an English country house mystery; *Deathtrap* does the same with the stage thriller itself. What mystery category has yet to receive similar treatment?

As a lawyer, I naturally thought of the courtroom drama. I'd read many great courtroom plays, but could not recall a single one that I would consider a modern stage thriller. What courtroom drama had a twist in the final moments of Act I that reversed the meaning of all the action to that point, followed by a second twist shortly into Act II that reversed the meaning of the Act I twist, and topped by an ironic but, in hindsight, inevitable twist at the end?

Even Agatha Christie's magnificent *Witness for the Prosecution* didn't qualify. While the Christie play has a phenomenal double twist at the end and a few nice surprises along the way, it lacks the major mind-bending middle twist that is a hallmark of the modern thriller. Structurally, *Witness for the Prosecution* is a traditional courtroom drama with an added double twist. That structure is patterned on a roller-coaster ride: first you're down, then you're up, then down again, then up again, and so forth.

What if somehow I could combine both structures in one play, the roller-coaster ride of a courtroom drama layered on top of a three-twist thriller? Wouldn't that be something original?

But I needed more than structural novelty; I needed a story that lent itself to my new structure. I had based *Seed of Doubt* on a real case from my days as a prosecutor; what other case could serve as my starting point?

There was only one candidate, and it involved an idea I'd had for some time. Almost twenty years earlier, we had prosecuted a young woman for murdering her lover's wife. Shortly into the trial, it became obvious that a member of the courtroom staff, a married man, was smitten with the very attractive defendant. We would joke that his wife should beware, given the defendant's recent past.

But what if he *wanted* to get rid of his wife, I'd mused to myself? What better way than to start an affair with an established wife-killer? Once the affair had begun, he could murder his wife and remain fairly certain that, while everyone familiar with those involved will blame him for his infidelity and poor judgment, they will blame the mistress for the murder.

There was a lot of circumstantial evidence against the defendant in our actual case, and her attorney kept claiming that all the evidence was forged, planted, etc. I don't remember if he ever actually used the word "framed," but that's what he meant. But what if the defendant were then accused of murdering a second lover's wife? Could she use the "framed" defense there, too?

Wouldn't the claim ring hollow the second time? Especially if it was rejected the first time?

For many years, a story had lingered on the edges of my consciousness. A lawyer representing a woman charged with murdering her lover's wife begins an affair with his client, convinces her to testify that she was framed for the murder, and then really does frame her when killing his own wife.

But how does he expect to get away with it? She is certain to point the finger at him. He's a logical suspect, too. What's his excuse? For the longest time, I had never pursued the idea further for this reason. Now I had to figure out sound answers to these questions. At least I had a perfect one-word title: *Framed*.

In searching for a solution to my plot problem, I thought a great deal about how pervasively the husband-murders-wife storyline dominated the genre. Worse still, in many of these plots, the husband had the flimsiest reasons for killing his wife. Take *Dial 'M' for Murder*, for example. Or (spoiler alert) *Deathtrap*. Why not do something else? And why not have a more compelling motive for murder?

In my view, the most compelling motive is self-preservation. X kills Y so that Y cannot destroy everything X has or holds dear. X doesn't seek gain; X seeks to maintain the status quo.

What if the husband isn't plotting to kill his wife, but rather someone threatening to reveal something explosive *about the husband to his wife* — something that will send the wheels of the husband's destruction into motion? Since the murder thwarts the disclosure, the husband would have no apparent motive to commit the crime. And if the victim were, say, the wife's sister, whom a stranger might mistake for the wife, then a stranger with a motive to kill the wife — like our wife-killing murder defendant — would be a far more logical suspect than the husband. The stranger could have mistaken the sister for the wife. But even if the husband had a motive against the wife, it is inconceivable he would have made the same mistake.

Mindful of theater economics, I pictured a very simple set: a lawyer's office represented only by a desk, a few chairs, and an oriental rug. Black curtains for walls. And for the non-office scenes, mostly in the courtroom, using the bare stage between the office set and the audience, with a chair or table brought on as needed. A minimalist design. We wouldn't even see the office's most notable feature — that the walls were covered with framed pictures, articles, magazine covers, and awards. That would be established through the dialogue. I even had the perfect opening lines (said to the lawyer by a colleague entering his office): "Do you frame everything? The frames alone must cost a fortune."

Yes, the title *Framed* now had a second meaning. Not only was it the lawyer's chosen defense for his client (to set up his own murder plan), but *Framed* also represented the kind of headline-driven, media-hound lawyer we often see on cable television.

In September 2008, I started mapping out Act I, describing each scene in reasonable detail and dropping in choice bits of dialogue. It began with the voices of three television reporters providing snippets of information about a local murder and the progress of its investigation, interrupted by brief interviews with

the neighbor who found the victim's body and the victim's griev-
ing husband (Mark), and culminating with the young female defendant (Jennifer) and her initial attorney (Murphy) standing center stage with the sound of cameras clicking, and Murphy saying,
"My client maintains her innocence. We have nothing more to say
at this time."

When the lights come back on, Murphy is entering the frame-
festooned office of his more celebrated colleague (Russo) to seek
Russo's assistance on Jennifer's case. They discuss the wealth of
evidence against her, and the likelihood of mounting a credible
defense. My Act I goal was to focus the audience on Jennifer's
case. Can any attorney get her off? Will Russo's chosen defense
— that the wealth of evidence against Jennifer had been planted
by Mark to frame her — work? What kind of witness will Jennifer
make when she testifies (as she must) that Mark framed her for
this crime? Are the pressures of the case driving Jennifer to cling
to Russo?

The action would alternate mainly between the office and the
courtroom, with a couple of inserts of Russo's wife (Diane) calling
from their home to establish the Russos' rocky marriage and Jennifer's knowledge of Diane's effect on her husband's peace of
mind.

At the end of Act I, Jennifer is lured to Russo's dark home. She
opens the door and turns on the lights, only to find a dead body
— looking like Diane but facing away from the audience. Jennifer
screams and runs out, whereupon we hear the reporters again describing this new crime, a new investigation, and Jennifer's sec-

ond arrest.

The final Act I moment puts Jennifer and Murphy again center stage, facing the press. Murphy again says, "My client maintains her innocence. We have nothing more to say at this time." But this time, Jennifer steps in front of her attorney to announce: "I've been framed!" Curtain.

It was a classic Act I twist. All along, we thought Russo was pursuing a "framed" defense to help Jennifer, and to show the rest of us that his deft courtroom skills were commensurate with his grandiose public image. Now we realize that he took Jennifer's case and chose this defense only for the most diabolical of reasons.

Act II begins in Russo's office in the aftermath of the murder — when, lo and behold, Diane walks in. Twist number two, reversing the meaning of twist number one. Diane's sister was murdered, not Diane. Jennifer had never met Diane. She knew Russo's wife only from an old picture on Russo's desk. Her mistake was understandable. Together with the other evidence Russo had arranged, all sides of the frame are solidly in place.

But what has Russo overlooked? What assumption has he made that would prove his undoing? Simple. Russo didn't design his defense for Jennifer because he believed it. He never believed it. He acted solely in his own interest. He assumed that the overwhelming mountain of evidence against her meant what it usually meant — that she was guilty. Indeed, his plan counted on the jury rejecting her first "framed" claim, so her second "framed" defense would never be believed.

I had to pull the rug out from under that assumption.

When the action shifts back to the courtroom, Murphy remains on Jennifer's case, having inherited the defense Russo committed Jennifer to pursue. I needed some credible evidence in Jennifer's favor. Murphy needed solid, persuasive grounds to argue that Mark, not Jennifer, shot Mark's wife. Unlike Russo, Murphy is a conscientious professional. If he must pursue this defense, he is going to do it diligently.

So I included the fact that the police report on the murder weapon states that, while Jennifer's gun was covered with her fingerprints, the ammunition had no prints, no smudges. Whoever loaded the gun was careful not to leave prints. As Jennifer had never been careful not to leave prints on the gun, did she load it?

Another piece of evidence against Jennifer was the record of a cellphone call around the time of the crime from Jennifer's phone (in the vicinity of the victim's house) to Mark's phone (in the vicinity of a restaurant where Mark supposedly was waiting for Jennifer). According to him, she called to say she'd be late. According to her, she made no call and wasn't late; they were supposed to meet a half-hour later.

Could Mark have hidden his phone in the restaurant to answer a call *he* made from his home, using Jennifer's phone? Looking through the settings on my own phone, I noticed something called "auto answer." If you turn this feature on, your phone will answer an incoming call automatically, after the number of rings you specify. Another point for Jennifer.

But I still needed something to cinch the case emphatically in Jennifer's favor. I've long found that when trying to fill a plot hole, look to a minor character you have underutilized. I had just such a person: the neighbor who had discovered the victim's body within minutes of the crime.

It was entirely logical that, after calling the police, she would try to phone Mark, the victim's husband. She tried three times. Each time, Mark's phone answered her call, but no one was there. Instead, all she could hear were the unmistakable sounds of a restaurant. Bingo!

Murphy sums up all of this evidence, and Jennifer is acquitted. Now there is a huge chink in Russo's plan. And yet, Jennifer's acquittal for killing Mark's wife does not prove Russo guilty of killing Diane's sister. I still needed an ending, and the final twist was eluding me.

It was February 2009. Half my year was over, and I hadn't written a word of the actual play. All I had was a detailed summary — without a finale.

One Saturday in February, I sat down to write out what I had so far. My summary was so detailed and my planning so thorough that I wrote the entire play (less the ending) that weekend. It was shorter than I had expected. I had consciously avoided any padding. In my heart, not a single line was superfluous.

Good thriller endings drip with irony. After an evening of characters convincing each other to believe what isn't true, *Sleuth* ends with one character refusing to believe the play's one truthful story, and paying a hefty price for his incredulity.

What would be an ironic way to prove Russo's guilt? Weeks passed, and I still had no answer.

Then one evening, I was driving home from work. I was making a left turn onto the entrance ramp to the highway when I had a revelation. No one proves Russo's guilt! The title of the play is *Framed*. Russo reaps what he sowed. Like Jennifer, he is framed for a crime he didn't commit!

All of the pieces fell into place in rapid succession. The police detective visits Diane and tells her his theory that Russo killed her sister. But he lacks proof. Did his sister keep any letters or a diary? Diana ostensibly refuses to believe the detective's premise. However, once he leaves, she rummages through her sister's possessions and finds the diary she knows her sister kept. It's locked, so she breaks it open with a letter opener. She reads it, begins to shake, drops the diary, and curses her husband. Then she notices the letter opener still in her hand, and gets an idea.

Russo had a very distinctive gold letter opener on his desk that he used prominently throughout the play. Now he enters his office and is about to attend to his mail when we hear his secretary's voice delivering a message that Mark (awaiting a murder charge for killing his wife) wants Russo to come to his home. As the light comes up on the apron of the stage, revealing Mark with Russo's distinctive letter opener through his chest, Russo picks up his mail and utters the play's final line, asking his secretary, "Did you see my letter opener?" Curtain. End of play.

I was very proud of myself.

I emailed the play to a friend who was an excellent sounding board for things like this. She read the play and thought it might benefit from expanding the final scene between Diane and the detective. Let the detective put the facts together more comprehensively, she advised, so that audience members who missed some of the subtler moments weren't left confused. The play needed more length, so I was happy to oblige.

Some additional tinkering followed. By the August submission deadline, I had completed the fourth draft. I pronounced *Framed* finished, sent it off to Owensboro, Kentucky, and waited.

One night shortly thereafter, I had a dream. I don't remember my dreams often, but this one I remember. I received a phone call from the International Mystery Writers' Festival telling me that, in their expert opinion, *Framed* was the greatest stage thriller that had ever been written.

I'm glad I don't believe in dreams.

The finalists for the 2010 Festival were supposed to be announced in February 2010. I confirmed that *Framed* had been received and was under consideration. There was nothing to do but wait.

February came and went, and there was no announcement. Now April was the target date. Furthermore, the Festival website posted that the 2010 edition would have only five finalists, not ten like in 2007 and 2008.

In May 2010, the word went out: the 2010 International Mystery Writers' Festival had been cancelled for lack of funding. All submissions for 2010 would be considered for 2011, as well as any additional submissions received by October 31, 2010.

More months of waiting followed, and then it was deja vu all over again — the 2011 Festival was cancelled for lack of funding. Everything was kicked over once again, to 2012.

I emailed the Festival organizers to try to find out whether *Framed* had ever been read and reviewed. Was it on the short list? If not, I wanted to begin submitting it elsewhere. If it was under serious consideration, however, I couldn't do that because other interest might disqualify the play from consideration in Kentucky, and the International Mystery Writers' Festival was a prestigious place for a stage thriller to get its start.

At long last, in February 2012, it was announced that the 2012 Festival was on. Many events were scheduled, but only one new stage play would be produced and performed. In April, the name of the chosen play was posted on the Festival website.

It wasn't *Framed*.

I won't dwell here on the play that was selected. When the Festival posted an audition notice for the play, there was a link to a copy of the script. I read it. Really?

A short postscript: The June 2012 International Mystery Writers' Festival was the last one held. In June 2013, the 2013 Festival was cancelled. Soon thereafter, Zev Buffman pulled up stakes and relocated to Tampa, Florida.

Truth be told, while waiting for the verdict from Owensboro, Kentucky, I had begun to sour on my play. It had a clever plot, decent characters, the courtroom scenes were fairly realistic, but the play essentially was meaningless. It wasn't about anything. It had a plot, but no story.

What's *Framed* really about? Isn't it about lawyers? Lawyers was a subject I knew well, having practiced law as a prosecutor and civil litigator for, by this time, over thirty years. What, specifically, about lawyers? There are two principal lawyers in the play, Russo and Murphy. What's their conflict? That's easy. Murphy focuses on the interests of his client; Russo is only interested in himself.

Most lawyers like to think they put their clients' interests first. But self-interest does tend to creep in. For example, lawyers are entitled to be paid for their work. If the clients don't pay, a law practice won't survive. All criminal defense attorneys insist upon payment up front, because they know they never will get paid once the case is over. Stories abound about the criminal defense lawyer, still waiting to be paid, who asks the judge to postpone the defendant's trial. When asked to justify his request, the lawyer says, "I'm trying to find my key witness, Your Honor." What witness is that, counselor? "Mr. Green, Your Honor." It's the code word for his fee. And since most judges once faced similar obstacles to the survival of their own practice, such requests are invariably granted.

Lawyers are also extremely mindful of their own reputations when handling a case. They know they will be appearing before this judge again; they don't want a reputation for making outlandish arguments (even if not, technically, frivolous) or shading the truth (even if not, technically, lying). They also know they will be dealing with opposing counsel again; they don't want to be known as someone who is impossible to work with. Why? Because this will hurt their ability to win arguments, and gain courtesies, in future cases. In other words, they may pull their punches slightly on behalf of their client today in order to benefit their client tomorrow.

And good publicity can make the difference between a high-priced lawyer and a common courthouse denizen. What lawyers don't keep one eye on the media when taking a case? They will say they are using the media to benefit their client's cause, and they are. But, face it, self-interest does play a part. At least a part.

I realized that my two lawyers, Russo and Murphy, represented extreme ends of this spectrum. Murphy was the opposite of slick. He wasn't a snappy dresser, didn't bloviate, and steered clear of trickery. He didn't like taking risks with his clients' lives. He would assess the evidence and proceed accordingly. He considered Jennifer's case unwinnable, and thought her interests best served by making a plea deal. He would get little out of this, but he wasn't the one who mattered.

Russo, on the other hand, rejected even the possibility of an unwinnable case. The more overwhelming the evidence he faced, the more he relied on theatrics to win. A trial was a show. The defendant and evidence were props. The jury was a flock of sheep to be herded. And the goal was a fat fee and another magazine cover for his office wall.

Who was right? Neither. As is so often the case, the right answer lay somewhere between the two extremes. And *Framed* showed that. If Murphy had had his way, Jennifer would have pleaded guilty. If Russo had pursued his strategy as he intended — a theory with no evidence to support it — Jennifer would have been convicted. Only when the two extremes worked in tandem did justice prevail.

Russo made Jennifer testify she'd been "framed" with no reason to believe it was true, thereby committing Murphy to continue with that defense. Murphy never would have made this claim on his own. Then again, Russo's actions also forced Murphy to do what Russo never would have done. Murphy diligently dug into the evidence to find the hidden nuggets that actually supported Russo's wild theory. Without the other, neither would have won. Jennifer needed both of them, each in his own way.

So what was *Framed* about? It was about two lawyers' different approaches to defending a murder case. One wants to achieve what he responsibly can for his client without taking any chances. But his risk-averse nature ties his hands and stifles his creativity. Meanwhile, the other looks at the case entirely through the prism of his own self-interest. He does not hesitate to gamble his client's fate on a highly imaginative yet risky defense when the potential personal reward is great enough.

In the summer of 2012, I took the play with me on our family's summer vacation. During those two weeks, I rewrote much of it, particularly the opening scene. I established the two types of lawyers much more clearly than in earlier drafts. This also added some needed length to the play. I still wanted to avoid padding, but in going over the play carefully, I noted a few instances where the action jumped from one scene to the next, and needed a smoother transition.

By the end of the summer, I had completed my sixth draft of the play. It was now 80 pages long, 28 pages longer than my first draft.

Enter my client Laith Nakli. Laith is an actor with a long list of film, television, and off-Broadway credits (including the Oscar-nominated film, *The Visitor*). He'd also written several screenplays, with a production team signing on to his most recent script. In time, he would write and star in the off-Broadway play *Shesh Yak* (Arabic for a 6-1 backgammon dice roll) at the Rattlestick Playwrights Theater, directed by Bruce McCarty. He is also the administrative director of the William Esper Studio, an acting studio on West 37th Street in Manhattan.

In one of our conversations, I mentioned to Laith that I had written a play. He offered to read it. In August 2012, I sent it to him. Two days later, he responded: "I read your play. Loved it. I couldn't stop reading it." He offered to put together a cast of excellent actors to read the play for me, so I could hear it performed.

The Esper Studio was constructing a 60-seat theater in its building so that its students could perform readings before an audience. When the construction was finished, Laith scheduled the reading for Friday night, June 14, 2013. Bruce McCarty agreed to direct. Laith gathered a group of Equity actors to participate, many of whom were Esper faculty members. They would read what was now the eighth draft of *Framed*, and rehearse the whole day preceding the evening reading.

I was excited, but also nervous as hell.

My wife, two kids, and sister went with me to the reading. Because this was the first reading in the Esper's new theater, the room was packed with Esper students. It was standing room only. Bruce gave a little introduction and told the audience who would be reading which part. Laith would read the stage directions. I was a bit surprised to see a male actor playing the neighbor, whom I had written as a woman but given a gender-neutral name (Terry). It was an important lesson in setting aside preconceptions when casting.

And then we were off to the races.

The three television reporters, whose interlocking voices begin the play, were written to sound like competitors, with each one trying to top the one before. Picture MSNBC, CNN, and Fox News. The cast handled that sequence magnificently. This started off the evening on a high note, and it was smooth sailing from there. Nothing surprised me. The play sounded from the stage exactly as it had sounded in my head.

My only disappointment was unavoidable. The ending of the play is very visual, and actors sitting in chairs could not possibly do it justice. But they made up for it with a coda that was not in my script. I had the reporters open and close Act I, but not appear again.   They brought the reporters back to end the play.   It worked.

The audience responded enthusiastically. Or maybe they were just being polite. I tried to engage Bruce in a discussion about how to improve the play, but he didn't have much to say. He made one suggestion: "You might want to add some theatricality. You might want to play with time." As examples, he mentioned two Lanford Wilson plays, *The Rimers of Eldritch* and *Book of Days.* He said he would send me copies, which he did.

"Play with time"? Could I deviate from a strict chronological account? Where to start? Once again I looked to something already in the play that was grossly underutilized: Diane's sister's diary. It already had occurred to me that the diary came out of nowhere. Not only did this give it something of a *deus ex machina* quality, but it also gave the audience no time to perceive its significance. What if there were a parallel narrative, something that happened after the action of the play ended, but shown while the play was in progress?

After Mark's murder, the police likely would obtain a search warrant for the Russo house, find the sister's diary, and read it. Why not show the detective on the side of the stage, in a spotlight, reading excerpts from the diary aloud throughout the play? The diary must be distinctive looking, with the clasp Diane broke dangling from the strap. And when I bring the reporters back at the end, just as the Esper actors had, I can finish with a news report that search warrants had been issued.

What should these excerpts say? I went through the play and found twelve spots where diary readings might be inserted. They had to be ambiguous. The audience should wonder whose diary this was. Diane's sister should never even be considered. So next to each spot, I noted which other characters could have written the entry: the murder victim, Jennifer, Diane. I also wrote down the theme of the entry, something that dovetailed with the action in the play at that moment. Then I wrote each entry. The last one, read aloud by the detective at the same time Diane is reading silently from an identical-looking diary, reveals the truth:

> How can I keep doing this to my own sister? And in her own house. Each night, he waits for her sedatives to take, and comes to my room. In the morning, I feel so guilty I want to hide under the covers. But I can't refuse him. What's wrong with me? I never wanted him this way. He's got to tell her. I've told him that over and over. He makes promises, then excuses. If he doesn't, I will. I've told him that, too. Any day now —

The diary entries worked on so many levels. They added mystery, they foreshadowed, and they made Russo's motive explicit rather than implicit. Draft number nine was 87 pages long, a good length. It was time to start submitting the play in earnest.

I started by researching all the theater companies in Westchester County, and especially the ones whose productions were reviewed regularly in the regional section of the Sunday *New York Times*. I located the relevant artistic director's contact information and sent an email inquiry. For some, I even managed to find the artistic director's personal email address. It's amazing what you can find online if you look hard enough. One had private students and a personal email address for that purpose. An aspiring actor listed another as a reference on a resumé, and provided the personal email address as contact information. Because serving as artistic director of a local theater is a part-time job, I couldn't count on their reading emails to their theater address. Occasionally, I received a response. Some offered to read the play.

Modern technology has made submitting plays much more convenient and less expensive than it used to be. In my formative playwriting days, I would have to go to a copy center, buy binders and mailers, and pay postage. Now I could email a pdf. I vowed never to send the play anywhere that didn't accept email submissions, or that charged a fee. Fortunately, the vast majority of theater companies have submission policies that seem to understand.

I also reached out to actor-writer-television host and commentator Charles Grodin, with whom I talked regularly because we were working together on a pro bono court case. I'd invited him to the Esper reading (but he couldn't make it), and to read the play. He said he didn't know much about mysteries, but his wife

(Elissa Durwood, a former critic with the *London Times Literary Supplement*) was a mystery writer and he would ask her to read it. A few days later, I received this email:

> Dear Rich,
> My wife read your play. She thought it was ingenious. I will send it to a few theater companies where friends run them. I often do this with my plays and there's a low percentage of them doing it but I'll give it a try for you.
> Best,
> Chuck

One of those companies was Primary Stages in New York City. A month later, I received an email from the artistic director. He acknowledged that Chuck had been "kind enough" to send him the play. Although he took a pass ("We are not able to do anything with the script at this time"), someone clearly had read it. His email included: "I enjoyed reading the play. The consistent twists and turns in the plot maintain a good level of suspense throughout. The characters are quite colorful. It's a good reveal when we find out that the diary actually belongs to [Diane's sister]. The intricate details of both cases are also executed well." He asked me to tell him if there were going to be any readings or workshops of the play in New York.

It still stands as my most detailed rejection. Usually you hear nothing or get a form response, which invariably begins by stating how many submissions were received. Clearly, someone felt the need to curry favor with Charles Grodin.

I also emailed the artistic director of the Vertigo Theatre in Calgary, Alberta, Canada, which specializes in stage thrillers. I received a response inviting me to send my play, emailed it off, but never heard anything further.

One Westchester theater, the Small Town Theatre Company in Armonk, New York, expressed some interest. I had seen their local production of *Twelve Angry Men*. It was a staged reading, where the actors moved about the stage with scripts in hand. When I spoke to the artistic director, I learned that all of their productions were staged readings. This allowed them to save rehearsal time and, thus, do more plays per year. He offered to arrange a private table reading of my play.

On October 29, 2013, he held the reading. It was very different from the Esper reading for two obvious reasons: the Esper actors were professionals, and the Esper reading had been rehearsed. This was a cold reading by amateurs. Experienced amateurs perhaps, but amateurs nonetheless. Notwithstanding, they did an excellent job. I was grateful to them, but the theater had no interest in taking the play to the next step.

I now scoured the daily postings on the nycplaywrights blog, and the monthly Play Submission Helper blog listings. Having created a synopsis document (complete with a list of the play's characters, its development history, and my bio) and drafted a cover email, I could submit *Framed* within minutes of reading what appeared to be a promising listing. And for free.

In the next nine months, I submitted *Framed* to 26 theaters around the country who were soliciting submissions and seemed an apt fit for the play. Most never responded.

One theater listing in particular caught my eye, because it included this sentence: "Be a comedy, drama, mystery, thriller or a monologue (no musicals or children's plays will be accepted)." It was the only listing I'd seen that expressly invited a "mystery" or "thriller." The theater was the Elite Theatre Company of Oxnard, California.

To submit a full-length play to the Elite, you first had to email a "letter of inquiry" summarizing the play, describing its cast and set requirements, and giving the play's prior history. Only unproduced, unpublished plays were eligible; every play had to qualify for a "World Premiere" in Oxnard. Prior readings didn't count.

Twelve days after my initial email, the Elite's artistic director, Tom Eubanks, responded, asking me to send the complete script: *Framed* draft number ten.

On October 15, 2014, Tom emailed me as follows:

> *Framed* got on my top-five list. I thoroughly enjoyed it. Unfortunately, to balance my season, I had to go with another play for our 2015 World Premiere production. I will automatically consider it again for 2016, so when I begin accepting submissions next year in March, I'll find out from you if it's been published or produced. If not, and you're willing, I'll consider it again. In the meantime, I hope you find a good home for it. It deserves a production.

It was the first positive feedback I'd received in a year. A few months later, *Framed* made the semi-finals at a theater in central Massachusetts, but not the finals. Otherwise, the emails went out, but nothing promising came back.

More months passed. I hadn't heard from Tom Eubanks in March 2015, as promised, and don't recall whether the Elite was still even in my thoughts.

On Thursday, November 5, 2015, I was working late in my office when I received Tom's email:

I'm considering *Framed* for our South Stage season in 2016. This is our smaller theater, which seats about 40-50. South Stage productions are generally new works and edgier plays that we might not include in our Main Stage season. First, has *Framed* been produced anywhere; if so, where? Second, would you agree to our producing the play for a short run of six performances on our South Stage in 2016; we pay $25 per performance on the Second Stage, and try our best to get you a review or two to aid in your future marketing of your play.

He included his cellphone number and invited me to call. I rushed home, told my wife, and took Tom up on his invitation. We had a great conversation. Tom is a private investigator by profession, and has spent much of his adult life in and around courthouses and the criminal justice system. One of the things he liked most about *Framed*, he said, was its authenticity. This had been one of my goals in writing the play — a play about lawyers that wouldn't make knowledgeable people cringe.

I accepted his offer. When I told Laith, he agreed completely. He saw it as "a great opportunity to build on getting your work produced" and said I "can slowly move from there."

According to Tom, the next steps were to find a director and schedule the play. There were three World Premieres slated for the South Stage in 2016, in March, May, and November. He didn't know yet which play would fill which slot.

As for the director, he had a roster of directors who worked regularly at the Elite. He might even direct himself (a possibility I encouraged, given his obvious affinity for the play). I was welcome to participate as much as I wanted. They might even be able to arrange for me to oversee auditions and rehearsals by Skype.

Once the director and slot were set, he would send me a contract. It is patterned, he said, on the standard Dramatists Guild agreement except in one respect. Given the Elite's circumstances, it is impractical to give the author approval rights over the director, cast, and set designer. I understood.

Frankly, I didn't care.

On December 1, 2015, I received an official notification from the Elite that *Framed* would run from May 7 through May 22, 2016, on Saturday afternoons at 2 p.m. and Sunday evenings at 7 p.m. Rehearsals were scheduled to begin March 28. Judy Blake had been chosen to direct. I was again encouraged to participate in the production, and the theater again reiterated its commitment to "make every effort to have your play reviewed by local reviewers for you to use in marketing your play for future productions with other theater companies." I was invited to attend all performances, but otherwise was given only one guest ticket. The Elite's Standard Production Agreement was enclosed, which I signed and returned.

Judy Blake contacted me three days later. She said she currently was directing a one-act play, but would be free to discuss *Framed* in January. In the interim, she was interested to hear my "reasons and motivations," that is, "how and why you came to write this play." I responded with the play's entire history: my long fascination with thrillers, the International Mystery Writers' Festival posting, the structural concept, the actual case upon which *Framed* was based, the 2012 rewrite, the changes made after the Esper reading — the whole shebang. I concluded: "For future reference, Russo was always played in my head by Al Pacino of the 1980's; the slick Al, not the scruffy Al. Murphy was more of a John C. Reilly type. Jennifer is early Mia Farrow. A younger Gena Rowlands would have made a good Diane."

According to what I could find online, Judy Blake was an experienced theater director up and down California, including for musicals. What I did not know at the time was that Judy had never before directed a new play or otherwise worked in tandem with a playwright. I was looking forward to collaborating with a director who suggested revisions, additions, cuts, and the like to improve the play. Judy was used to accepting a play as it appeared on the page.

On December 23, the Elite's website announced its three South Stage productions for 2016. *Framed* was described exactly as I had prescribed. Describing a thriller can be a delicate business. You have to hook the audience without giving anything away. For this reason, I've always been very protective of any description of the play, and the theater respected that.

Next to the description was a stock photo of a pile of law books with a gavel on top, and the typewritten word "Framed" superimposed across the photo in yellow. It was not the best logo.

That night I designed on my computer how I wanted my play branded: a row of three identical, antique picture frames on a wall, with the letters "FR," "AM," and "ED" in each frame, respectively. It represented the essence of the play, not only frames on a wall, but also three frames specifically, to symbolize the three frames that took place during the play: Mark framing Jennifer, Russo framing Jennifer, and Diane framing Russo. I sent the logo off to Tom who promptly had it swapped for the books-and-gavel.

Judy and I exchanged some emails in January and February. She envisioned no major rewriting, welcomed my thoughts on casting and the set, and indicated that auditions were scheduled for March 21. She also asked my plans for coming to Oxnard.

I told her that I had planned to be there from May 1 through May 8 — the last week of rehearsals and the first two performances — but hoped to stay in close touch in the interim, mentioning Tom's earlier Skype reference.

In early March, an audition notice was posted, including "sides" for each role. I quickly wrote to Tom and Judy to point out that the detective's "sides" were only of him reading diary entries, not speaking his own lines; I suggest some alternate dialogue from Act I (as publicly posting the detective's Act II dialogues would give away too much of the plot). In addition, the notice's description of Murphy was a bit misleading. Was I nitpicking? Perhaps. Perhaps I risked getting on their nerves. But I thought it vital to ensure that *they* were not misunderstanding the characters, or if they were, that it be corrected as soon and clearly as possible.

All casting would occur through the open auditions. Judy had reached out to one "excellent actor" beforehand, and given him a copy of the play, but nothing had come of that. I tried to engage her in a discussion of whom we should be looking for, but she thought it best simply to see the candidates and select the best and most suitable for each role. I had hoped to participate by Skype but, a week before the auditions, was told this was not possible according to the theater's technical director. Nevertheless, Judy promised to discuss the auditions with me before making any final casting decisions.

In November, when I first discussed *Framed* with Tom Eubanks, I asked whether the Elite was a "community theater" or a "regional theater." It was a relevant question if *Framed* proved worthy of consideration for a "best play" Edgar. There aren't many new stage thrillers annually, and I regarded *Framed* of comparable merit to recent Edgar winners. However, eligibility required at least a regional theater production.

Tom rejected the distinction. As far as he was concerned, all theaters where you must pay for a seat are the same.

Certainly when it comes to casting, they are not all the same. In community theater, you get what you get. The actors are usually quite experienced, but many tend to be older which makes casting younger roles problematic. And community theater is a second-shift endeavor. Auditions and rehearsals are in the evening, after the regular work day. There is no certainty how many people will show up and, therefore, how much choice you will have.

At my request, auditioning actors provided digital photos of themselves, which Judy emailed to me. Few looked the parts as I had grown to picture them. Most were, let's say, "grayer" than I expected. Yet several had professional credentials, and I found some listed on the Internet Movie Database.

Judy's email indicated that she was very happy with the actors she'd found for every role but Mark. From the photos alone, I tried to anticipate her choices but, when we spoke by phone the next day, learned I was wrong on every count.

I was especially troubled by Judy's casting of Russo. Russo is all about appearances, and her choice didn't project that appearance.   She described him as having a slight English accent, but Russo is a hustler, not a gentleman.

In anticipation of the first table read, I asked Judy if I could listen in by speakerphone. She preferred I didn't; she wanted to be alone with the cast, and would give me a rundown afterwards. Then I found out that her initial choice for Russo had backed out due to a scheduling conflict, and Alexander Schottky had now been cast in the role. I looked up Alexander online. *He* had the look I wanted. I watched his Oscar Mayer commercial. If he could credibly hustle bacon, he could credibly hustle Jennifer.

Judy reported that the table read had gone well. She had given the cast my account of how *Framed* came to be written, which they appreciated. They did ask to change the name of the restaurant in the play (the "Wagon Wheel," named after an upscale but long-closed Westchester restaurant, the Water Wheel). Apparently, "Wagon Wheel" was the name of an actual restaurant near Oxnard. I had no objection. (It became "Park Hill.")

She also asked about the reporters. What had the Esper actors done that I liked so much? I said that Bruce McCarty clearly had taken the stage direction "overlapping, competing" to heart, with each reporter trying to top the one before. As I pointed out, I had written each set of three reports so that the second is slightly more sensational and tabloid-like than the first, with the third pushing the envelope even further.

Within days of the table read, the role of Mark was cast and the entire cast was now set. Rehearsals were underway, and there was little more I could do to help. So I turned my attention to publicizing the play.

My goal was not advertising the play in the conventional sense; it was to ensure that the play would be reviewed by the local press. Finishing this experience with a tangible acknowledgement of my work was of enormous importance to me. Good reviews lead to further productions, but you can't get good reviews if reviewers don't attend. Tom always had said that the theater would try its best to get reviewers to see the play, but there were no guarantees.

How could I make a review more likely? My idea was to do a "Sunday piece." I had grown up reading numerous such articles in the "Arts & Leisure" section of the *The New York Times* on the Sunday before the Broadway opening of a play or musical, usually accompanied by an Al Hirschfeld pen-and-ink caricature (with the name of his daughter Nina hidden in the folds of a gown or as strands of hair, among other places). More specifically, in my ongoing research on stage thrillers, I had found several feature articles in newspapers around the country, usually accompanying the revival of classic thriller, asking the where-have-all-the-thrillers-gone question.

My piece was entitled "At Long Last, a New Stage Thriller,"[1] and it explored why "a genre that remains so popular now [is] so rare," concluding that "the simple answer to why more stage thrillers aren't written is that they're damn hard to write!" It explored the challenging requirements of the genre, my own challenges writing *Framed*, and concluded with a teaser about the play.

---

[1] *See p. 151.*

I didn't give away too much information for, as I wrote, "With a thriller, you must hook your audience using as little bait as possible. Spoil the surprises, spoil the play."

I sent the piece off to Tom who liked it very much, but thought its 1,235 words probably too long for publication. Nonetheless, he passed it on to the Elite's marketing director who posted it on the Elite's website, and also sent it to the local newspapers. Of course, putting it on the website effectively precluded a newspaper publication, but Tom always felt this was unlikely. To compensate, he contacted several reviewers personally, asking them to come see *Framed*. There was nothing more I could do. Until May 7, I would just have to hope.

Then things started to happen that made me regret being 2,841 miles away from where my play was being rehearsed. Apparently, the cast expressed confusion over the sequence of events in the play. With the diary readings, I had "played with time," as Bruce McCarty had recommended — and now no one could assume that the *rest* of the play was told in chronological order, as it was.

Act I ends with Jennifer's trial testimony, followed by Russo framing her for murder. Her testimony doesn't end her trial, however; that doesn't happen until the middle of Act II, after Murphy develops the fingerprint and cellphone evidence supporting her innocence.

The ordering of these events is essential to the logic of the plot. Russo needs someone who cried "framed" previously. He cannot implement frame number two until *after* Jennifer testifies (and personally proclaims frame number one), and he must do it *before* her trial is over (when he assumes Jennifer will be convicted, jailed, and unable to serve as his patsy).

Evidently, the cast thought that Jennifer's testimony ended her trial, and that the trial scenes in Act II related to the second crime (even though their subject matter — the neighbor who found the body, the cellphone call, and the restaurant rendezvous — clearly refer to the first murder).

Furthermore, Act II includes two scenes in Russo's office where the detective questions Russo, one before Jennifer's acquittal and one after. In my quest to cut any excess dialogue from the script, I began the second of these two scene with the detective already in the office, and repeating a theme raised during their first encounter.

The cast found this confusing, too. Was this all one scene, interrupted by some kind of flashback to an earlier trial? Shouldn't these scenes be reordered to join the two halves of the Russo-detective scene together?

I tried to explain to Judy the meaning of the entire sequence. Tom also weighed in, agreeing that the running order was integral to the plot. Judy didn't dispute this; her focus was on eliminating confusion. If the cast is confused, the audience is sure to be confused. It was a fair concern, and I had an idea how to fix it.

A few extra lines scattered throughout the play solved the problem. Following Jennifer's testimony, in a brief scene where Russo reassures her ("Don't worry about it. These things happen. What's done is done.") and invites her to his home (with its dead body), I added that "the trial isn't over. The trial isn't close to being over. Jennifer, you were only our first witness." Similar new material early in Act II underscored that the second murder interrupted an ongoing trial that was far from complete.

As for the two Russo-detective scenes, I added one sentence to the detective's opening lines in the second of these scene. He now began, "Remember, on my last visit, we discussed . . ." This was enough to clarify that these were separate encounters, not one continuous one.

With all changes highlighted, I sent Judy my eleventh draft of *Framed*. But the exchange concerned me. Judy hadn't brought this "confusion" to my attention until I reached out to her for an update. Were there other problems I wasn't hearing about? It was April 10. I wouldn't be in Oxnard for another three weeks, when it might be too late to make any significant changes. Judy would respond promptly to my questions, but rarely initiated contact. I brought my concerns to Tom's attention, who tried to reassure me without disclosing his private conversations with Judy.

I also starting giving thought to other potential areas of confusion. Would the audience wonder how the detective got his hands on the diary? Was the play's final reference to a "search warrant" too obscure?

What if the detective doesn't start the play on stage reading the diary, but enters (from where Diane would later find the diary) holding the diary at the corners with a handkerchief (as a detective finding evidence might), studying its cover, strap, and broken clasp, flipping through its pages — and only then arrives at the spot where he will be reading the excerpts and begins. Then, during the final reporter sequence at the end of Act II, he duplicates the identical business with the diary -- entering from the same side, repeating the action exactly, and arriving at the same spot as the play ends. Wouldn't the repetition convey to the audience that he found the diary at the end of the play, and thus didn't start to read it until after the rest of the play had ended?

Judy and I discussed the idea. She persuaded me that the audience had enough information to process in the opening moments. This additional piece wouldn't register or, even worse, might suggest that the diary was found at the beginning of the play. That would be disastrous.

The final diary business, however, might be an effective visual ending to accompany the voices of the reporters. She even suggested ending the play with the detective rereading the entry that begins the play. But it wasn't necessary to decide any of this now, she said, so we put it on hold.

Meanwhile, Judy brought a few other issues to my attention. In my script, Jennifer had met Mark, a plastic surgeon, when she saw him professionally about breast augmentation surgery — and fell for him when he dissuaded her from having the operation, telling her she was beautiful just the way she was. Given the casting of Jennifer, it no longer was realistic that she would be seeing a plastic surgeon for this reason, so I changed the reason to fixing a (barely visible) bump on her nose.

In making this change, I also rewrote the ending to show exactly how adding the detective and diary under the final reporters' voices would work. I did not include a further diary reading; the addition was entirely visual. It was draft number twelve.

Judy also asked about proper court attire for attorneys. Was a sport coat okay? Not in court, I said, and certainly not for the prosecutor.

These were the easy questions. Others were more problematic. After Diane's sister is murdered, Diane refers to Jennifer once as "she." Can we change "she" to "Jennifer"? No. Diane would never refer to the woman she believes murdered her sister as "Jennifer." "She" remained.

Another proposed change would have compromised the key dramatic moment early in Act II when it's revealed that Diane's sister, not Diane, was the Act I victim. It's a three-step revelation: first, with a message from Russo's secretary over the office inter-com; second, with Russo's exit lines; and third, when Russo reen-ters seconds later with Diane. Due to "constraints of the stage," I was asked to drop Russo's exit, and let Diane enter alone. But Russo's exit is important. It punctuates his final question, and leaves Murphy to answer his question to an empty room. What "constraint" wouldn't allow this? What "constraint" permits Di-ane to enter, but not Russo and Diane, one after the other? To bet-ter understand, I asked to see a photo of the set, but was told the set wasn't finished. The change request was then withdrawn.

However, I was growing increasingly frustrated with the process. I welcomed, and had cooperated with, constructive revi-sions. But too often I was presented with undesirable proposed changes for reasons that were unexplained. I didn't enjoy being the burr under everyone's saddle, but no one else seemed to be defending the integrity of my play.

On April 22, Judy sent on an email she had received from a member of the cast, claiming to have found four "contradictions" in Murphy's summation at the end of Jennifer's trial. I addressed each of the four, and reminded Judy that, aside from writing the play, I also had decades of experience with criminal trials. Murphy argued his case exactly as a real attorney would have presented it. Didn't anyone trust that I knew what I was writing about?

I also asked Judy if she had tried my new ending: the detective finding the diary under the final reporters' voices. She said it was a question of whether I wanted to end with a "bang" or an "ah-ha" moment. She also confirmed that all sound effects in the script (police sirens, clicking cameras, door sounds, a cellphone's ring, drawers opening and closing) were in place, and invited me to select the music I wanted to open and close each act.

This was something I'd never considered before. After much thought, I chose a segment from *Rhapsody in Blue* to open Act I, a bit of *Claire de Lune* to open Act II, and the second movement of Beethoven's Ninth Symphony to close each act.

It was April 29. My wife and I were flying to Bob Hope Airport in Burbank, and from there, driving to Oxnard, in two days. Before leaving, I sent an email to Tom Eubanks soliciting his take on the current state of the play.

Tom responded that he had watched the entire rehearsal the previous evening, had some concerns about the mood and style of the performance, but knew how to fix the problem and was discussing the solution with Judy (although he didn't rule out speaking directly to the actors). When I pressed him for details, he declined to disclose his conversations with Judy, saying only that "there are specific scenes that are not being played in a way that I believe you intended."

It was a less-than-satisfying response. I didn't want to pry into private conversations, or appear not to appreciate the delicacy of the theater's artistic director questioning the work of my play's director, but why should either assume my intentions when I was available to tell them directly.

To Tom, my intentions were clear. *Framed* was a realistic mystery, not a melodrama. That's why he chose it for the Elite. He wanted to correct some scenes in Act II that were playing "superficially and melodramatically," and therefore losing their "emotional payoffs."

I told Tom that I had complete faith in him, wished him well, and started to pack for California.

If you want to find the perfect accommodations, wherever you travel, talk to my wife. She's the undisputed champion at locating the ideal vacation rental. For our Oxnard trip, she found a well-appointed one-bedroom condominium available for the week of May 1-8 on Peninsula Road in Oxnard, a short walk from the Elite Theatre.

We arrived Sunday evening. No activity was planned until late Monday afternoon when, in advance of the regular 6:00 p.m. rehearsal, Judy would be working with several actors on specific scenes starting at 3:30 p.m.

I arrived at the theater a few minutes early. The first thing I noticed was the black, white, and red *Framed* banner hanging on the outside wall. The logo wasn't the one I designed, which I attributed to economics: my design used more than three colors. [Tom later told me this wasn't the reason. The Elite staffer who commissioned the *Framed* banner, poster, and palm card from the Elite's regular designer, and sent the designer's work to the printer, never knew a logo already existed. The oversight was rectified in time to use my logo on the programs.]

Judy greeted me warmly and began showing me around. She took me into the theater to show me the set. I learned that the Elite had gone to considerable expense to modify the South Stage for *Framed*. The proscenium had been extended several feet, a step down from the main stage, for all of the non-office scenes. It was just like my script described. Passageways also had been added behind the set and on each side to allow for entrances from both stage right and stage left.

However, in one critical respect, the set contradicted my script. Russo's office had walls. My script said explicitly: "The walls are all left to the imagination." I did that for a reason. Not only did it save space and production cost, and thus make the play more attractive to small theaters, but an essential symbol of *Framed* is that Russo's office walls are covered in picture frames. With no walls, the frames can be implied. With walls, those walls *must* be covered with frames.

These walls had some frames, but not nearly enough. Many clearly had been created with great care. There was a mock *Forbes* magazine cover with the words "Power Player" over a large photo of Alexander Schottky, the actor playing Russo; and a "Thomas Russo" Supreme Court admission certificate. But there also was a lot of bare wall space. Judy assured me that they had purchased many additional frames and that the walls would be full by the opening. It was a distraction my script had tried to avoid. [Judy and Tom both told me that they read my script's language to mean that the walls were left to *the set designer's* imagination. It seemed an odd interpretation, especially in light of my mid-February email exchange with Judy in which I described the office set as furniture "against a black background (no walls, no windows)."]

Minutes later, Alexander (Russo) and Nancy Solomons (Diane) appeared and began rehearsing their scene together near the beginning of Act II. Initially, Judy would turn to me during each break either to ask a question or gauge my reaction. This bothered

Nancy. Actors want clear direction from one director. They don't want mixed messages from multiple sources. It was an important lesson for a newly produced playwright. From that point on, I confined my comments to the production team, and only spoke to the actors if one of them asked me a direct question.

After an hour with Alexander and Nancy, Ken Johnson (playing the detective) walked in. He and Nancy began rehearsing their long, late scene — the one that explained the case to the audience. It was a difficult scene for both actors. For Ken, there was a lot of dialogue to remember, and this was giving him difficulty. For Nancy, she needed something to do during the scene, and the script didn't provide anything. Judy proposed that Nancy work on a jigsaw puzzle. In this way, she can show her disdain for the detective's theory by turning her attention to the puzzle. And it had symbolic value, as the scene culminated with the detective's admission that his theory lacked a vital "missing piece."

Ken is a gray-haired, dignified actor with a polished, baritone speaking voice. It was the perfect voice to read the diary entries. His acting style also reminded me very much of John Williams' Inspector Hubbard in *Dial 'M' for Murder* (a performance with which Ken was unfamiliar). I had pictured a gruffer character, but Ken's portrayal worked equally well.

At six o'clock, the full rehearsal began. The cast performed the play from beginning to end without interruption. Judy took careful notes; I took some as well. At the end of the run-through, Judy gave her notes to the actors (whom she addressed by their character's name). I served principally as technical advisor. Alexander put his hands in his pants pockets during the courtroom scenes. That's a no-no. So was the dark gray shirt Jake Mailey, as the prosecutor, was wearing. Jake also brandished a key piece of documentary evidence from his jacket pocket. Put it in a folder, Jake.

And then there was Jennifer's trial testimony. The first part, the direct examination, is a series of snippets from her presumably longer testimony. We hear no questions, just her answers. Jennifer answers, the lights dim and come back, she gives another answer, the lights dim and come back, and so forth. To enhance the discontinuity, Olivia Heulitt (Jennifer) shifted her position in the witness chair between each statement. She also crossed and recrossed her legs. Her attorney would have instructed her not to do that.

These were small points but, by the same token, they were also small corrections that gave the scenes greater authenticity.

The bigger problem was the ending. The South Stage has limited lighting options. There is a powerful spotlight, but that was being used exclusively for the detective's diary readings. The other light was from above and, even though different sections of the stage had their own lights, these lights bled into other sections. In other words, you couldn't black out one section completely while using another.

In the script, Mark's body lies in darkness until midway through Russo's final office scene, and then is shown while Russo completes his lines. That didn't work here. You could see Mark's body throughout. To avoid this, Judy tried Russo's first half without Mark on stage, then dimmed *all* the lights while Johnny Avila

(Mark) took his place, and brought the lights back up for Russo's finish. It was very awkward. I suggested swapping the order so that Russo finishes his entire scene, then the stage goes black and the lights come back up on Mark's body.

The scene required Johnny to do a lot very quickly in darkness. The ending only worked if the audience recognized the letter opener in Mark's chest as the one they'd seen Russo use in his office. It had to be positioned to catch the audience's eye. Chris Bryson, playing the neighbor, donated a very ornate gold letter opener, a replica of a Byzantine dagger, but it was not overly large.

One morning, my wife and I toured the antique and collectibles shops in Ventura looking for a bigger gold opener, and concluded that Chris' was much larger than anything else available. I suggested adding a few lines of dialogue in Act I about the Byzantine opener, to call specific attention to it. Judy didn't think it necessary and felt it interrupted the flow of the scene. Instead, she asked Alexander and Larry Swartz (our first-rate Murphy) to find a few more opportunities to handle the opener in Russo's office scenes, to make it as recognizable as possible.

Undeniably, the final moments of the play are complicated. A lot happens. Diane leaves the stage to find her sister's diary, reads the diary silently (as the detective reads it aloud), decides to take revenge on her husband, and fixates on a letter opener as the means to do so; Russo discovers his letter opener missing and we find it in Mark's chest; the reporters report another murder; and the detective finds the diary. It would take much of the final week to work out the timing of all these elements.

During Monday's rehearsal, Judy tried her idea of ending the play with the detective repeating his first diary reading. It didn't work for me. As I told Judy, "I don't want the audience wondering if the play is ever going to end — which was a little of my reaction." We cut it.

There were other issues as well. Several sound effects selected before my arrival weren't very good. For example, when characters face the press during the reporters sequences, the audience is supposed to hear the "rapid clicking of cameras." All I heard was the repeated clicking of one camera. I went online and found a "paparazzi cameras" effect that sounded much better. There also was a "closet rummaging" effect that improved upon the indistinct sound of Diane opening and closing drawers, looking for the diary. The production team made these changes.

And then there was the matter of getting Alexander on stage at the beginning of Act I. The initial sequences on the apron of the stage used lights that bled into Russo's office, so there had to be a pause to dim the lights and let Alexander enter and take his place behind Russo's desk. That pause interrupted the continuity of the action. Judy suggested reducing the length of the blackout by having Alexander hide behind his desk, and pop up quickly at the right moment. Alexander went along reluctantly, and breathed a sigh of relief when this alternative didn't work either.

I had this suggestion: let Alexander sit at the desk throughout, reading a newspaper. So what if the audience sees him. He's reading about Mark's wife's murder. He's following the case, thinking how he can use it to his own advantage. Problem solved.

I tried to be helpful where I could. Ken was still having problems remembering his lines during his scene with Nancy. He can carry a notepad and pen, I suggested to Judy. Detectives carry notepads. He can, too. He can use the notepad as a memory aid.

At Wednesday's technical rehearsal, along with ensuring the correct lighting and sound cues, Tom started taking a more active role in staging the final moments of each act. He worked with Olivia on her discovery of the body in the Russo home. Instead of one scream, he wanted her to scream twice. Tom also worked with Nancy and Ken on their scene, and with Johnny on Mark's final moments. Tom put Mark in a chair, rather than on the floor, so the audience would have a better view of the letter opener.

And then illness descended. Olivia, who worked with kids, started getting a sore throat so begged off screaming during rehearsals. Nancy needed emergency dental care and missed some rehearsal time. But the worst illness befell Ken, who was now home in bed. I offered to read his lines from the front row during rehearsals, but when someone suggested that I fill in on stage if Ken was too sick for the opening performance, I politely declined. I'm not an actor. Modern medicine stood a better chance of bailing us out than I did.

There was some good news. Alexander had a close friend, a professional videographer, who volunteered to record the first performance — if I agreed. I did, as long as it was understood that no one would post the full video online and, if actors wanted to put together a clip reel, that it would not be distributed publicly without speaking to me first (to make sure they weren't giving away the twists in the play).

Thursday was the final rehearsal (because of the Friday evening performance of *Men of Tortuga* across the lobby on the Main Stage). Ken still was out of action. Tom continued to work on key scenes with Nancy and Johnny. The play wasn't perfect, but nothing ever is.

My final request was that someone take responsibility for filling the stack of unused picture frames (with random newspaper articles, if necessary) and putting them on the walls. The stage manager already had discovered that the glass on the existing frames was reflecting the lights, and had removed all the glass and glued the contents to the backing of each frame.

Friday afternoon brought more good news. Ken was still sick but he was coming to the opening. And theater critic Jim Spencer of the *Ventura Breeze* was coming, too.

Tom invited my wife and me to attending the Friday performance of *Men of Tortuga* as the theater's guests. We were up early Saturday morning because *Framed* producer Vivien Latham had arranged for Alexander, Larry, Nancy, and I to make a guest appearance on the "Tom and Kat" radio show on KVTA in Ventura to promote the play. We were supposed to go on between 8:00 and 9:00 a.m., but had to wait until the show was almost over at ten o'clock. It was a wham-bam-thank-you-ma'am interview, followed by Alexander and Larry reading a short scene. Host Tom Hilton seemed more interested in why the Elite Theatre Company didn't spell "Theatre" t-h-e-a-t-e-r.

The opening was now four hours away.

We arrived at the theater about an hour before the 2:00 p.m. curtain. I first checked on the number of picture frames on the Russo office walls. It was much improved, although the set still did not exude the unbridled egomania I had envisioned (and had hoped to convey with words and no walls). Also in the theater was Alexander's friend, setting up his state-of-the-art video camera. He didn't know the play, so the logical camera location was a fixed position that could take in the entire stage. Hopefully, the high-definition resolution would be crisp enough that, in an edited version, one might zoom in closer and cut between different sections of the stage. We found the ideal spot for his camera and his microphone.

In the lobby, the cast was gathering, Ken included. He looked worn but ready. Volunteers were setting up one table for refreshments and another for selling raffle tickets. A bronze statue of Sherlock Holmes was a key Act I prop, but had taxed the production budget (and was unlikely to see much future use in the prop room). So the Elite decided to raffle it off. The winner could collect the statue at the end of *Frame*'s run.

Three of my wife's cousins, who lived near Oxnard, arrived. They were happy to see us, but knew enough to leave me alone as I braced for the moment of truth. Tom pointed Jim Spencer of the *Ventura Breeze* out to me, adding that Jim not only was a critic but also a practicing lawyer. This was great news. I hoped the play's realism would impress him.

Judy and I wished each other well, took seats together in the back row, and I turned my cellphone off. The South Stage was practically full by two o'clock, when the Elite's doors were closed and locked, and a black curtain drawn across the entranceway. This was necessary to keep the bright daylight out of the theater during the play.

The opening strains of *Rhapsody in Blue* filled the South Stage, and Ken stepped into the spotlight to read the first diary entry. Magically, I was instantly transformed from someone who wrote plays to be read silently, to someone who wrote plays to be performed before an audience.

The first act went very well. Ken had taken my suggestion and brought a small notepad which he referred to even on the witness stand, as police witnesses often do. There were a few minor mistakes but nothing noticeable.

Intermission is when things took a bit of a turn. I switched my cellphone back on to see a bunch of frantic messages from one of my law partners. Her husband and brother, both of whom I knew well, had flown from New York to Los Angeles for the sole purpose of seeing my play. They had flown in Saturday morning and were planning to fly back Saturday night. Arriving at the theater forty minutes early, they decided to walk across the parking lot to get something to eat and when they returned, found the doors locked. They tried to contact me repeatedly for help, but my phone was off. After flying coast-to-coast and getting there on time, they had missed Act I.

It took me a few minutes to adjust my mind to the fact that

these guys actually committed to travel nearly six thousand miles in one day to see *any* play in Oxnard, California. After greeting them, thanking them for coming, and apologizing for what had happened, I tried to explain the story to this point, which was difficult. I invited them to stay over for Sunday's performance, but Sunday was Mother's Day and they had to get back. Ultimately, I emailed each of them a copy of the script to read on the flight home. I don't know if either did — but both certainly did show me their support.

The distraction was such that I never noticed that the solid wooden armchair placed at the extreme left of the apron to serve as the witness chair for all the courtroom scenes in Act I and the first half of Act II, had been moved during intermission to stage right. This wasn't supposed to occur until midway through Act II, in time for Nancy to use it when working on her jigsaw puzzle in her long scene with Ken.

But the detective and neighbor still had key courtroom testimony in Act II. Ken entered to find no witness chair. So he stood, British courtroom style. As did Chris. What else could they do?

Ken clearly was tired. In his long scene with Nancy, even with a notepad in hand he had great difficulty remembering his lines. She tried to cue him while staying in character, a few exchanges were in the wrong order, but they powered through it.

The complex final sequence went as well as could expected under the circumstance. It wasn't as I had written it. That vision was abandoned when we realized that the South Stage's lighting constraints wouldn't permit my original ending. I looked forward to another opportunity to do the play free of these restrictions.

The house responded enthusiastically to *Framed*.   No one shouted, "Author, author!" but, at the conclusion of the curtain call, Alexander introduced me and Judy to the audience.   Nor was there a gala opening night party at Sardi's to await the verdict of the critics.   Instead, once the audience filed out, my wife's cousin bought a string of raffle tickets, our guests popped open a bottle of champagne outside, and then we retired to a quiet family dinner. I was done until the next night at 7:00 p.m.

Because of Mother's Day, they weren't expecting a large Sunday audience. Accordingly, the Elite decided to give each cast and crew member free passes for friends and family.   The big Sunday news was that Rita Moran, the *Ventura County Star*'s theater critic, also would be there. *Framed* was getting two reviews.

Before Sunday's performance, Alexander told me that he had received and watched the video.   He asked when I was leaving, and invited me to his home the next morning to collect a copy.

Tom introduced me to his wife, whom he described as a big mystery fan. So it was especially satisfying to overhear her during intermission discussing the first act — with no doubt that Russo had framed Jennifer *for the murder of Diane*.

The second night of *Framed* went better than the opening. Ken was feeling much better, with a lot more stamina — and was letter perfect. The witness chair stayed where it belonged. I even noticed a smile on Rita Moran's face as she left the theater. Had she enjoyed the play? Or was she looking forward to the scathing review she was planning to write?

When the theater emptied Sunday, my work in Oxnard was done. I gave my thanks and said my farewells to everyone involved. The next day, my wife and I went to a Best Buy, bought an external hard drive, went to Alexander's house, and he transferred a copy of the video. Later that day, we flew home.

On Wednesday, May 11, Jim Spencer's review appeared in the *Ventura Breeze*.[2] It was everything I reasonably could have wished for. He said, "The script is engaging, entertaining, highly credible, and well worth your time," and that "the script bears an uncommon authenticity, as well as being literate, concise and cogent."

This was the magic combination I had been trying to achieve since 2008. "Entertaining" and "engaging" while also "highly credible" with an "uncommon authenticity." "Cogent" — meaning logical — while also "literate." And "concise," that is, without the padding I had always tried to avoid.

His only criticism concerned the ending: "It is presented abruptly, almost without warning, and then the curtain falls. Boom! The show is over. In our view the audience is not given enough time to fully take in what happened before the house lights come up." If only he could have seen my original ending.

Tragically, Jim died less than five months later at the age of 74 from a swiftly-moving inoperable brain tumor. People have said that gratitude can be undying. If so, Jim has mine.

Two days later, on Friday morning, Rita Moran's review appeared.[3] I had been warned that Rita tended to summarize a play

---

[2] See p. 155.

[3] See p. 157.

more than critique it, and her review bore that out. Nevertheless, the banner headline over her review said enough: "Whodunit '*Framed*' will keep audience guessing." [That was the print headline. The online review was headed: "Elite Theatre's '*Framed*' offers a killer performance that will keep audience guessing."]

The reviews worked. Saturday the theater was full. Sunday was standing room only. The next day, Tom emailed me saying, "The show is doing fabulous and folks are enjoying it very much." He wanted to extend the run another week. The cast agreed to the extra performances. I gave my consent. What an enormous coup. As Tom pointed out, I could now boast that "due to popular demand, *Framed*'s World Premiere was extended." Not to mention the additional raffle tickets they could sell.

Tom offered another $50 royalty check, but I traded the royalty for free tickets for my two college-aged kids and my sister, who were flying out for the May 21 Saturday afternoon performance.

Alexander had emailed me to make sure my family arrived early. The South Stage does not have reserved seating and the theater was overbooked. In fact, almost twice as many tickets were sold than seats. My son texted me that the start was delayed while more chairs were brought into the theater. According to Judy, "The audience was enthralled and showed it," there was "laughter in all the right places," with "the audience audibly discovering each little nuance and clue" and giving "heartfelt applause." My daughter described how everyone gasped at the key moments.

I was so pleased that this was the performance my kids and

sister got to see.

Before the final performance on May 29, I emailed the cast and crew thanking them all for their dedication and hard work. "Because of you," I said, " I can now call myself a 'playwright' without putting any modifiers in front." I promised to let them know if *Framed* found a life after the Elite.

Tom Eubanks sent the following response:

> *Framed* was a hit. *Framed* was entertaining, intriguing and made audiences think about the process and culture of our legal system. No play on our South Stage has received the standing-room-only audience numbers that *Framed* delivered.

> Having you here for the week leading into opening was a real benefit to the entire production. Although that is the most challenging week for an opening play — a new play especially — it was a real pleasure having you here, getting to meet you and your wife and getting to know you as playwright.

> I hope you'll find many theaters that will find in your play what I did and produce it. Thank you for honoring Elite Theatre Company with the World Premiere of *Framed*.

And I was awed and honored by Tom's words. But the most surprising news was yet to come: My wife's cousin won the Sherlock Holmes statue.

Even before the Elite run was over, I started planning for *Framed*'s next life. First, I went through the script carefully fixing some lines that I thought could be improved. Though I believed my original ending would have alleviated Jim Spencer's concern, I nonetheless added a little bit of business to draw out the final moments of the play and make it even clearer that Russo's gold letter opener had been used.

But the biggest change was to the long scene with Diane and the detective. Judy had been absolutely correct that Diane needed something to do while the detective explained his theory. And sending Diane offstage to find her sister's diary, and having her return with both the diary and her chrome letter opener, was hard for the audience to follow.

I had a brainstorm. If Diane's sister was staying in the Russo home, she must have brought clothes. When the detective enters, Diane should be folding and packing her clothes in two suitcases, one closed and standing, the other open on the floor. She should keep folding and putting clothes in the second suitcase while the detective is speaking, stopping only when impelled by something he says.

The payoff comes after the detective exits. Instead of Diane leaving the stage (and our hearing a sound effect of someone rummaging in drawers or a closet), Diane remembers that she packed her sister's diary *in the closed suitcase*. She retrieves it *without leaving the stage*. But she can't open the diary, so she exits only momentarily to get the letter opener (underscoring the letter opener because she gets it separately).

With the play still running at the Elite, I made these changes to the script. It was *Framed*'s thirteenth draft.[4] I joked with Tom and Judy that they needn't implement these changes until after they moved *Framed* to the Elite's Main Stage, with its more sophisticated lighting grid, for an unlimited engagement.

Then I began compiling a list of possible avenues to explore. This included regional theaters that had passed on *Framed* before but, when presented with *Framed*'s two reviews and track record of consistent SRO performances, might be willing to take a second look. I also asked everyone I knew if *they* knew anyone who might prove helpful. They responded with the names of two Broadway producers, a producer's associate going out on her own, and the managing director of a major regional theater — and agreed to reach out on my behalf.

On the off-chance that a month-long run at the Elite might make *Framed* eligible for Edgar consideration, I contacted the Mystery Writers of America — only to learn that the "best play" Edgar no longer was being awarded. There weren't enough contenders.

Knowing England's affinity for stage thrillers, I even explored opportunities "across the pond."

Nothing led to anything. And to make matters worse, the Elite production made *Framed* ineligible for most submission opportunities, available only to unproduced, unpublished plays.

The Elite Theatre Company's production of *Framed* did make

---

[4] *See p. 73.*

me eligible for full membership in the Dramatists Guild. I took the *Framed* video, edited it down to a two-minute trailer and, with the permission of the two actors in the trailer, posted it on my Dramatists Guild member page, along with links to the two *Framed* reviews.

I've continued to write and submit other plays. Maybe one of these will catch on. But *Framed* is my favorite. It deserves more.

This is not to denigrate my Oxnard experience. I was produced once. No one can take that away from me. The Elite's poster for *Framed* hangs — professionally framed under museum glass (to protect it from fading) — on my office wall. The frame for the poster cost more than the $150 I earned from the production. I also have a box of leftover material from the Oxnard run that the Elite kindly mailed me, at my request, after the play closed.

Then I had an idea. The book that inspired me to start writing plays was Moss Hart's brilliant autobiography *Act One*, with its detailed account of the creation of Hart's first hit, *Once in a Lifetime*. Every fifteen years or so, I would take my copy of *Act One* off the shelf and reread it.

Why not write a book about my one success after 40 years trying to become a produced playwright? It's no *Act One*, but it's a decent story.

And maybe, just maybe ...

FRAMED

A Thriller in Two Acts

By Richard Weill

FRAMED was first presented by Vivien Latham and Stephanie Rice at the Elite Theatre Company in Oxnard, California on May 7, 2016. It was directed by Judy Blake; the set was designed by Ms. Blake; costumes were by Sheryl Jo Bedal; and the lighting by Pat Lawler. The cast, in order of appearance, was as follows:

GEORGE OLIVETTI	Ken Johnson
TERRY SANDERSON	Chris Bryson
MARK LOWERY	Johnny Avila
EUGENE MURPHY	Larry Swartz
JENNIFER CREIGHTON	Olivia Heulitt
THOMAS RUSSO	Alexander Schottky
DIANE RUSSO	Nancy Solomons
PROSECUTOR	Jake Mailey

OFFSTAGE VOICES: three television reporters, a judge, and a secretary

TIME

The present.

SETTING

Most of the action takes place in THOMAS RUSSO's law office, represented only by a fine wooden desk and leather chair, two additional leather chairs on either side of a lamp table, and an oriental rug between the desk and the table. The walls are all left to the audience's imagination.

On RUSSO's desk is a telephone, a old, framed picture of his wife Diane as a young woman, and a gold-plated letter opener.

Downstage of RUSSO's office is a wide area of bare stage that serves as portions of a courtroom, crime scenes, and RUSSO's home. At most, a table and one or two chairs will be used for the action in this area, which can be brought on as needed. In the text, this section of the stage is referred to as the "FRONT AREA."

If facilities permit, the area of the stage representing THOMAS RUSSO's office may be elevated several inches above the FRONT AREA, but this is entirely optional.

ACT I

*(A spotlight shines on GEORGE OLIVET-
TI standing to the right of the FRONT
AREA. He is holding a distinctive-looking
DIARY. It is covered in bright red leather
with a diagonal white stripe running from
the upper right corner of the front cover to
the lower left corner of the back cover, bisect-
ing the spine. The red leather strap that
once locked the DIARY closed now hangs
free, its clasp broken. OLIVETTI skims
some of the DIARY's contents, and then
reads aloud.)*

OLIVETTI

He doesn't look at me the way he used to. His eyes used to light
up when I walked into the room. Now he looks away. Is it me he
doesn't want to see — or is he afraid his eyes will betray a guilty
conscience?

*(The light fades on OLIVETTI, followed by the sound of a
police siren. A spotlight shines on the lifeless body of a
WOMAN in the center of the FRONT AREA. She is facing
away from the audience. She is a brunette.)*

VOICE of FIRST TV REPORTER

This upscale community was rocked last night by the discovery of
thirty-six-year-old Christine Lowery, found dead inside her home.

VOICE of SECOND TV REPORTER
(Overlapping, competing.)

Neighbors were stunned to learn of the shooting within sight of
their own front doors.

VOICE of THIRD TV REPORTER
(Overlapping. Another competitor.)

A real-life Nightmare on Elm Street as the thirty-six-year-old wife
of a local surgeon is found murdered in her home.

(OLIVETTI, no longer carrying the DIARY, approaches the WOMAN's body.)

VOICE of FIRST TV REPORTER
(Overlapping.)
Police say that the victim was speaking on the telephone with a neighbor when someone came to her door.

(OLIVETTI reaches into his pocket, removes a pair of surgical gloves, and puts them on.)

VOICE of SECOND TV REPORTER
(Overlapping.)
Lowery put the caller on hold to go greet her apparent killer.

(OLIVETTI begins to examine the WOMAN's body.)

VOICE of THIRD TV REPORTER
(Overlapping.)
She opened the door and never was seen or heard alive again.

(The light fades on OLIVETTI and the WOMAN. Spotlight on TERRY SANDERSON, standing to the right in the FRONT AREA.)

SANDERSON
When Christine didn't pick up again, I tried to call her back. I — I kept getting a busy signal, so I went to her house. The door was open. There she was.

VOICE of FIRST TV REPORTER
The neighbor, Terry Sanderson, is not considered a suspect.

VOICE of SECOND TV REPORTER
(Overlapping.)
Police do not consider Sanderson a suspect.

VOICE of THIRD TV REPORTER
(Overlapping.)
Sanderson is not considered a suspect at this time, but the investigation is continuing.

VOICE of FIRST TV REPORTER

The police are investigating the whereabouts of the victim's husband, Dr. Mark Lowery, at the time of the crime.

VOICE of SECOND TV REPORTER

(Overlapping.)

Dr. Lowery is a well-known plastic surgeon.

VOICE of THIRD TV REPORTER

(Overlapping.)

Lowery has a long list of celebrity patients, mostly women.

(Spotlight on MARK LOWERY, standing to the left in the FRONT AREA. The rapid clicking of cameras can be heard.)

LOWERY

I'm happy to cooperate in any way I can. My only goal is to find out who did this terrible thing to my wife.

VOICE of FIRST TV REPORTER

Police sources now say there is evidence that Dr. Lowery, the victim's husband, was elsewhere at the time of the murder.

VOICE of SECOND TV REPORTER

(Overlapping.)

A new twist in the Lowery murder investigation. It seems that Dr. Lowery has an alibi.

VOICE of THIRD TV REPORTER

(Overlapping.)

Forensic evidence has now linked a new suspect, a former patient of Dr. Lowery, to the scene of the crime.

VOICE of FIRST TV REPORTER

(Overlapping.)

Twenty-eight-year-old Jennifer Creighton has been charged with the murder of Christine Lowery.

(Spotlight on JENNIFER CREIGHTON and EUGENE MURPHY, standing in the center of the FRONT AREA. The sound of cameras clicking is now louder.)

                              VOICE of SECOND TV REPORTER
          (Overlapping.)
Police say Ms. Creighton had a relationship with Dr. Mark Lowery.

                                    MURPHY
My client maintains her innocence. We have nothing more to say
at this time.

                              VOICE of THIRD TV REPORTER
According to police, clear and convincing evidence establishes
Creighton's commission of this crime.

          *(Spotlight on OLIVETTI standing at the right of the FRONT
          AREA. He is reading from the DIARY.)*

                                    OLIVETTI
I'm tired of sharing him. I don't care who he says he really loves, I
still want him all to myself. It doesn't have to be this way. I won't
let it.

          *(The FRONT AREA darkens and the lights come up on
          THOMAS RUSSO's office.   RUSSO stands at his desk,
          comparing a stack of dress shirts and an array of ties. MUR-
          PHY enters carrying a briefcase.)*

                                    MURPHY
          *(As he puts the briefcase down, takes off his coat, revealing a
          dull brown suit and colorful tie, and places the coat over a
          leather chair.)*
Do you frame everything? You're running out of wall space in
your waiting room.

                                    RUSSO
All glory is fleeting. People need to be reminded.

                                    MURPHY
          (Looking at the "fourth wall.")
Not to mention in here. The frames alone must cost a fortune.

RUSSO

You should see the men's room.   We put the latest articles in a glass case over the urinals, so you have something to read while you're standing there.

MURPHY

You're kidding, right?

RUSSO
(Continuing his examination of the array of shirts and ties.)
Look for yourself.

MURPHY

Is this a bad time?

RUSSO

I'm on T.V. this afternoon.   They want opinions on why the woman in Arizona was acquitted. Or was it Oklahoma?
(Holding up a shirt and two ties.)
Which tie goes better with this shirt?
(Spotting MURPHY's suit and tie.)
Maybe you're not the best guy to ask.

MURPHY

It was Oklahoma. The acquittal.

RUSSO

Doesn't matter. Wherever it is, they ask the same questions, and I give the same answers. "Why was she acquitted?" "Because in America, you can't be convicted of a crime unless the prosecution proves your guilt beyond a reasonable doubt."   And then I pray for the follow-up: "But wait a minute — didn't she confess to the crime, and weren't there eighteen eyewitnesses who saw her do it, and didn't she leave a trail of DNA a mile wide, and wasn't the murder caught on video?"   And I say, "Yes, but remember — there's a difference between being innocent and being 'not guilty.' You don't have to be innocent to be 'not guilty.' In fact, you can be *probably* guilty. But, obviously, all that evidence didn't make her guilty beyond a reasonable doubt."

MURPHY

Before you wrap that Oklahoma jury in the American flag, I suggest you listen to the foreman's press conference. As he tells it,
their reasons were fairly jaw-dropping.

> *(Having selected a shirt, RUSSO picks up the gold letter*
> *opener on his desk and starts to remove the tags and wrap-*
> *ping.)*

RUSSO

I don't care if they voted "not guilty" because they thought it was
Election Day and that was the name of their congressman.   I'm
doing a defense attorney's second most important job.

MURPHY

Self-promotion.

RUSSO

Raising the bar. Bit by bit, case by case. So that *my* jury, in *my* next
case, will look at the evidence there and say, "Hey, there's less evidence here than there was in that case in Arizona, or Oklahoma.
So if she wasn't guilty there, I guess that means I have to acquit
here, too."

MURPHY

Not exactly the Lord's work.

RUSSO

We each worship in our own way.   You'll see.   This Creighton
case'll teach you. Win the press, win the case.

MURPHY

Not on Creighton.   The press is my worst enemy on Creighton.
It's making everybody dig their heels in.   If there were a way to
kill the coverage —

RUSSO

You can't. Not for a case like this. Anyway, the trick is *getting* the
coverage, not killing it.   Why would you kill it?   Creighton is
every defense attorney's holy grail.   Woman shoots her lover's
wife? No, *rich* woman shoots her lover's wife. You can write your

own ticket after a case like that.

                    MURPHY
She's not rich. Her father is.

                    RUSSO
Even better. A father who neglects his family for his business.
Who now blames himself for his daughter's situation. Guaran-
teed, he gives you a blank check.

                    MURPHY
I still need a defense. "My client maintains her innocence" only
goes so far.

                    RUSSO
Then find one.

                    MURPHY
I've tried. If she'll tell me that Lowery planned the whole thing,
and *made* her do whatever she did, I would play for a lesser con-
viction on some diminished mental capacity. Or offer a plea deal
in exchange for her cooperation. But she keeps denying everything. And the D.A.'s not going to agree to any deal if the case
stays a front-page story. I need a way to kill this coverage.

                    RUSSO
Diminished capacity? Cooperation? What kind of victory is that?
If you're going to blame the husband, blame the husband. Go all
the way.

                    MURPHY
It's not credible. The victim's blood splatter is on Jennifer's shoe.
Fibers in the pool of blood at the house are from Jennifer's clothing — clothing where they also found gunshot residue. Her
whereabouts are unaccounted for at the time of the crime. And
the weapon is probably hers.

                    RUSSO
"Probably"? Either it is, or it isn't, or the test is inconclusive —
which effectively means it isn't.

MURPHY

It hasn't been tested, because it hasn't been found. But it will be. At least, I can't count on the fact that it won't be.

RUSSO

Gene, you've been sitting at the poker table your whole career getting dealt a pair of fives, a pair of eights. Now, suddenly, you're dealt four queens. It's a once-in-a-lifetime hand. Milk every last dollar out of it while you still can.

MURPHY

That's crazy talk. Four queens. What kind of deck are you playing with? The prosecutor's got the cards, not me.

RUSSO

And you want to kill the publicity. Use the publicity! Get out there. Proclaim her innocence. Point the finger of guilt at somebody else. Give the prosecution something to be nervous about.

MURPHY

It's a bad idea. It's a bluff. In the long run, it'll do her more harm than good.

RUSSO

You know what I think? I think you're not ready for the big time. You're not ready for the spotlight.

MURPHY

This isn't about the spotlight, Tom. It's not supposed to be about me. It's supposed to be about her. I think, to you, the spotlight's the only thing that matters. You're a fucking moth.

RUSSO

Don't start getting all high-and-mighty with me. You're no different than I am. Where do you get your business? From cops, right? Cops recommend you. Cops hand out your cards in the lock-up. "Trust me, call this guy. Not a fancy dresser, but he's honest, and he's good." And do you ever trash the cops to get a guy off? Never. Because it's bad for business. Because it's biting the hand that feeds you.

MURPHY

Because it's bullshit. Because it's usually a cheap shot at decent guys doing a job.

RUSSO

Spoken like a true Irishman. No, because it's bad for business. Well, I get my business by getting my picture in the paper. That's the monster I gotta feed. So I feed it.

MURPHY

Well, this time you're trying to feed it my client.

RUSSO

I'm trying to save your client. You're trying to quietly ship her up the river while no one is paying attention.

MURPHY

I don't have a choice.

RUSSO

Sure you do.

MURPHY

The evidence shows that —

RUSSO

The evidence shows whatever you make it show!

MURPHY

No, the evidence shows what the evidence shows.

RUSSO

Yeah? Really? When a witness points the finger of guilt at some-body, do you take that at face value?

MURPHY

Shoes don't lie.

RUSSO

They don't? If whoever wore them — or carried them — is lying, then the shoes are lying. Evidence doesn't always point. Sometimes it's *pointed.*

MURPHY
(After a beat.)
Does this shit ever work?

RUSSO
With juries? Absolutely. Where do you think jurors get their view of the world? From the *Harvard Law Review*? From television. Where the obvious is never true, where the most likely suspect never did it, and where the real truth isn't revealed until ten minutes before the final credits.

MURPHY
They're not that stupid.

RUSSO
No comment. But it's conditioning, not stupidity. And every couple of months, thank God, they show *Twelve Angry Men* on television again to reinforce the conditioning. Man, I love that movie. When Henry Fonda sticks that switchblade into the jury table —
(Demonstrates with his gold-plated letter opener, using his desk.)
— and says, "It's possible. Isn't it possible?" Of course, it's possible! Because everything's possible. Because this is America, the land of possibilities. We've been conditioned to believe that, too. And when those two beliefs come together — that anything's possible, and possible means innocent — all I can say is: it's wonderful.

MURPHY
That's not the law, and you know it.

RUSSO
Hey, it's not my job to disabuse people of everything they've come to believe. It's not my job to tell them there is no Santa Claus. And I'll tell you another secret.

MURPHY
What's that?

RUSSO

They're also conditioned to accept the most outlandish story if —
and this is critical — if it's told to them by someone who truly believes it. Or sounds like he does. How do you think I win my
cases?

MURPHY

By being selective.

RUSSO

Bullshit.

MURPHY

By not taking unwinnable cases.

RUSSO

There's no such thing as an unwinnable case — if you've got balls.
Balls is the answer.

MURPHY

When asked his view of legal ethics, Mr. Russo replied, "Balls."

RUSSO

It's unethical to present false evidence. It's not unethical to paint
whatever ballsy picture you want from the evidence that's already
there. Or, more importantly, to fill in the blank spots, where there
is no evidence, with balls.

MURPHY

It's taking an unacceptable risk with someone else's life.

RUSSO

You gotta take chances in life. You gotta bet big to win big.

MURPHY

It's not your money.

RUSSO

It's your reputation. Do you want to be known for getting people
off, or getting them convicted of some other crime?

MURPHY
I want to be known for doing a top quality, professional job.

RUSSO
Jesus. No wonder the cops recommend you. You're their kind of lawyer.

MURPHY
My priority is my client, not the glass case over my urinal.

RUSSO
And I don't? Serve my client? My reputation, my public image goes nowhere but down unless I deliver for *them*.

MURPHY
But you need some facts to work with.

RUSSO
They're already here.   A woman murders her lover's wife? Doesn't that sound a bit fishy to you? A cheating *husband* murders his wife — that makes sense.

MURPHY
They investigated the husband. He was their number one suspect for a long time.

RUSSO
They gave up too easily.

MURPHY
He has a rock solid alibi for the time of the crime.

RUSSO
Nothing is rock solid. There's always doubt — until ten minutes before the credits, remember?

MURPHY
And if he didn't have an alibi, and if they'd charged him instead, you'd now be saying just the opposite.

RUSSO

If I was representing him, you're damn right I would.

MURPHY

Some things are true.

RUSSO

Did anyone see Jennifer Creighton shoot Christine Lowery?

MURPHY

No.

RUSSO

Has Jennifer Creighton admitted killing Christine Lowery?

MURPHY

I wouldn't let the police question her.

RUSSO

Did she admit it to you?

MURPHY

As I said, she denies everything. But I haven't pressed her about the details.

RUSSO

Of course you haven't. You may be conventional, but you're not dumb. Because deep down you don't want the truth to tie your hands either.

MURPHY

It's too soon.

RUSSO

Yeah? But not too soon to discuss her diminished mental capacity, or her testifying that Dr. Lowery made her do it — both of which presuppose her admitting her guilt.

MURPHY

I haven't discussed those with her either. They were just some thoughts I had.

RUSSO

Well, they're the wrong thoughts. You're defending a circumstantial case with no eyewitnesses and no defendant admissions and a client who maintains her innocence, you're ready to throw in the towel, and *I'm* crazy?

MURPHY

There's scientific evidence. Corroborated several times over. You talk about jurors getting their ideas from television? This is the stuff they eat up.

RUSSO

Yeah? Convince me. Convince me that Jennifer Creighton murdered Christine Lowery.

MURPHY

All right. First, the victim makes a seven-oh-five p.m. call to her neighbor, Terry Sanderson. Sanderson discovers the body at seven-twenty and immediately calls the police. So the crime was in that fifteen minute window. Jennifer and Mark Lowery were supposed to meet at the Wagon Wheel Restaurant at seven. Lowery showed on time but Jennifer didn't show until seven-thirty. That's strike one.

RUSSO

So she was late.

MURPHY

She wasn't. Jennifer says she thought the appointment was for seven-thirty, not seven. The police think Jennifer told Lowery to be there at seven to give him an alibi.

RUSSO

Why?

MURPHY

Because, otherwise, he'd be charged. He's the most likely suspect — and it wouldn't do Jennifer any good to eliminate the wife in order to get the husband, only to have the husband wind up in prison.

RUSSO

That's nothing but speculation.

MURPHY

Now the gun. The victim was shot twice with a thirty-two. The police infer it was a revolver because they found no shell casings. Jennifer owns a thirty-two revolver. I know that. The police may not. Not yet anyway. Because it's unlicensed.

RUSSO

And they haven't found it.

MURPHY

Not yet. They searched her place. Jennifer insists she didn't use it, or let anyone else use it. I haven't asked her where it is.

RUSSO

Don't.
(With a chuckle.)
She might actually tell you.

MURPHY

Exactly. But it's somewhere. And that's strike two.

RUSSO

That's strike nothing. It's not proof. Just more speculation.

MURPHY

You want me to bet Jennifer Creighton's life on that? On something so tenuous, that could change in an instant?

VOICE of SECRETARY
(On an intercom.)
Mr. Russo, your wife's on line one.

RUSSO
(To MURPHY.)
Hold on. I gotta take this.
(Picks up phone.)
Thank you.
(Pushes button on phone.)

What now, Diane?

> *(Spotlight on DIANE RUSSO standing in the FRONT AREA, holding a telephone receiver.)*

DIANE

Did you see my keys?

RUSSO

No.

DIANE

I can't find my keys.

RUSSO

So?

DIANE

Without my keys, I can't go out.

RUSSO

Are you going out?

DIANE

I might.

RUSSO

Really? When's the last time you went out?
> *(A long pause.)*

Then I really can't be bothered. Ask Marianela. Gotta go. Bye.
> *(Hangs up. The light fades on DIANE. To MURPHY.)*

Sorry about that. If I don't take the call, she keeps calling.

MURPHY

How's she doing?

RUSSO

Who, Diane? Mezza mezza. It's a rollercoaster ride between histrionics and disfunction.

MURPHY

That's too bad.

RUSSO

They warn you to look at the mother before marrying the daughter, and her mother's a total fruitcake.   Communicates only through the dog. "Tell Cookie all about your day."

MURPHY

I'm sorry.

RUSSO

You didn't do anything.

MURPHY

Are you ready for strike three? The scientific evidence?

RUSSO

Go ahead.

MURPHY

Police recovered Jennifer's scarf. The victim's blood splatter was on it, as well as gunshot residue. At the crime scene were fibers, in the victim's blood, that match the scarf. There's also a spot of the victim's blood on one of Jennifer's shoes.

RUSSO

Did you ask her if anyone had access to her clothes, her property?

MURPHY

Yeah. She doesn't know. Jennifer's not real organized.

RUSSO

I know the type. Believe me, I know the type.

MURPHY

Do you see what I've been saying?

RUSSO

I'm not convinced. Everything you've described — the gun, the scarf, the shoe, the appointment at the restaurant — could have been set up by the husband.

MURPHY
You expect me to get up and yell, "We wuz framed"?

RUSSO
Maybe. If that's what it takes. If that's what will sell.

MURPHY
You're nuts.

RUSSO
You want *me* to do it?

MURPHY
You're trying to take over my case.

RUSSO
Not take over. Join the defense team. I'm sure Daddy Creighton
will have no objections.

MURPHY
However you word it, it's still taking over my case.

RUSSO
You don't seem to believe your client. I'm willing to.

MURPHY
You're going to destroy any chance she has.

RUSSO
Why don't we let her decide?

MURPHY
She's confused enough as it is.

RUSSO
It's her life, as you keep saying.   I'd like to meet Jennifer
Creighton.

(The lights fade on RUSSO's office. Spotlight on OLIVETTI

standing at the right of the FRONT AREA. He is reading from the DIARY.)

OLIVETTI

He doesn't belong to her. He belongs to me. She's not his soul-mate. Not like I am.

(The light changes to JENNIFER and MURPHY standing in the FRONT AREA, side by side. The PROSECUTOR stands a short distance away. They are in court.)

MURPHY

Your Honor, Ms. Creighton has no criminal record. She has deep roots in this community, and frankly has nowhere else to go.

PROSECUTOR

That's a ridiculous statement given her father's wealth, Your Honor. Someone with access to five hundred million dollars can always find a place to go.

MURPHY

Her father is willing to post a substantial amount of bail on her behalf to guarantee her presence. I ask that reasonable bail be granted.

(The lights fade on JENNIFER, MURPHY, and the PROSE-CUTOR.)

VOICE of JUDGE

The court sets bail in the amount of one million dollars.

(Spotlight on OLIVETTI standing at the right of the FRONT AREA. He is reading from the DIARY.)

OLIVETTI

I'm entitled to this. Nothing else makes sense.

(The light fades on OLIVETTI and rise on RUSSO's office. RUSSO sits at his desk. MURPHY and JENNIFER also sit.)

                    RUSSO

Whatever you tell us, Jennifer, is confidential.

                    JENNIFER

Okay.

                    RUSSO

But there's a catch I must warn you about. Under the law, we're not allowed to present any evidence we know isn't true. Not suspect, not believe, but know. So if you were to tell us that the reason you were a half-hour late to the Wagon Wheel Restaurant was that a flying saucer landed in the parking lot, just as you were parking your car, and little green men took you to another planet, served you a bowl of my mother's minestrone, and then brought you back — all in thirty minutes — we're allowed to let you testify to that. It probably wouldn't be very smart of us, but we're allowed to do it because, crazy as it sounds, we don't know it's not true. Follow me so far?

                    JENNIFER

I think so.

                    RUSSO

However, if you were to tell us that you shot Christine Lowery at seven-ten —

                    JENNIFER

I didn't.

                    RUSSO

Just as an example — *if* you were to tell us this, and then we were to find a witness who swears that he was with you from seven to seven-thirty p.m., in that flying saucer in another galaxy, that he in fact sprinkled the grated parmesan cheese on your minestrone, we couldn't call that witness to testify, even if we wanted to. Because we know — from what *you've* told us — that this witness isn't telling the truth. So, while we need for you to tell us what happened, you must know before we start that what you tell us can restrict what evidence we can introduce in your defense. Are we straight about that?

JENNIFER

That's not a problem. I didn't do anything wrong.

RUSSO

Everyone does things that are wrong, Jennifer. Accepting a married man's dinner invitation, to many people, is wrong.

JENNIFER

But we —

RUSSO

(Cutting her off.)

But fortunately, I don't deal in right and wrong. I'm not here to judge the morality of your life. I deal in guilty and not guilty. If I can find a reasonable doubt in your favor, that's all I care about.

JENNIFER

I'm just saying —

RUSSO

And I'm just saying that the fewer extra things you tell us, the better. Let me decide what I want to know. I will ask you questions. Answer my questions. Only my questions. Okay?

JENNIFER

Okay.

RUSSO

Good. Now tell us why you were late to the Wagon Wheel.

JENNIFER

I wasn't late. Mark told me to meet him there at seven-thirty.

RUSSO

You're sure?

JENNIFER

I'm sure.

RUSSO

How long have you known Dr. Lowery?

JENNIFER

Six months.

RUSSO

How did you meet?

JENNIFER

I made an appointment. I wanted him to fix my nose. I've always been very self-conscious about my bump.
            (Turning to profile and pointing.)
See?

RUSSO

            (He doesn't.)
I'll take your word for it. Weren't you unhappy with Dr. Lowery?

JENNIFER

Why?

RUSSO

That apparently your bump is still there.

JENNIFER

No, you don't understand. Mark wouldn't operate. He told me I was beautiful just as I was. He told me all the things he saw in me, things no one had ever said before.

RUSSO

Good for him.

JENNIFER

He changed my life.

RUSSO

I'll bet he did.

JENNIFER

Yes.

RUSSO

Tell me about the scarf and shoes the police found. Did anyone else wear them? Did anyone else have access to them?

JENNIFER

I don't think so.

RUSSO

Does anyone else have a key to your apartment?

JENNIFER

Just my parents.

RUSSO

No neighbors, no hide-a-key box anywhere?

JENNIFER

Yes. On the hide-a-key box. It's hidden in the laundry room of my building.

RUSSO

Does anyone else know it's there?

JENNIFER

No. Except Mark. I was with him once when I got locked out. He helped me get the spare. But it couldn't have been him.

RUSSO

Why not?

JENNIFER

Mark's a warm, loving man. He's soulful. He wouldn't hurt any-one.

RUSSO

Look, Jennifer, this is a circumstantial case. That means that no one saw who did it, and no one has admitted doing it. The way you ordinarily defend against a circumstantial case is to show that the prosecution's evidence can be interpreted in several different ways. Maybe the scarf fibers were in the Lowery house because you used to visit there. Or the gunshot residue was on the scarf because you wore it to go duck hunting. Or you got blood on your shoe and dropped fibers on the bloodstained carpet because you walked into the house after the crime and panicked.

                    JENNIFER
I see.

                    RUSSO
But none of this will work here.

                    JENNIFER
Oh.

                    RUSSO
No. And you know why not?

                    JENNIFER
No.

                    RUSSO
Because, minutes later, you met Mark at the Wagon Wheel and said nothing. So there's no ordinary explanation for the blood and fiber evidence, at least none any normal person would believe.

                    JENNIFER
I see.

                    RUSSO
Another way to defend a circumstantial case is to challenge the scientific evidence. It isn't Christine Lowery's blood on your scarf and shoes, it's yours — or it's the blood of someone who'd had an accident, and you stopped to help. You prove that a thousand identical scarves were sold within a fifty mile radius of the crime scene in the last two years.

                    JENNIFER
Okay.

                    RUSSO
Twenty years ago that defense might have worked, but it doesn't anymore. The science has become too sophisticated.

JENNIFER

I see.

RUSSO

And you can't suddenly say she attacked you first and you were just defending yourself.   She was in her own home, and, once again, you said nothing about it to anyone when you got to the Wagon Wheel.

JENNIFER

You're making me nervous.

RUSSO

That's understandable — and since nervous is a far cry from insane, we really aren't left with much to work with here.

JENNIFER

What are you saying?

RUSSO

I'm saying that if you wish to maintain your innocence, we're left with only one possible defense: That the reason your scarf fibers are there and the victim's blood is on your shoe and all the rest is because someone else put them there deliberately, to make it look like you killed Christine Lowery.

JENNIFER

Who would do something like that?

RUSSO

The one person who had a motive to eliminate Christine Lowery. Mark Lowery.

JENNIFER

Mark wouldn't. He just wouldn't.

MURPHY

Eliminate Christine in order to be with Jennifer — and also frame Jennifer?

RUSSO
(To MURPHY.)
You and I can discuss the details later.

MURPHY
Seems kinda self-defeating, doesn't it?

RUSSO
I said later.

MURPHY
Jennifer is entitled to know where you're going with this.

RUSSO
All right.   Jennifer, it's time you faced an unpleasant fact.   Mark
Lowery is neither warm nor loving.   He's a killer.

JENNIFER
No. I don't believe it.

RUSSO
Killing his wife and framing you wouldn't defeat his plan. It *was*
his plan. He wanted to be free of both of you. He wanted to be
free to pursue numerous relationships, so he killed the proverbial
two birds with one stone. He *used* you. He saw you as someone
suggestible enough to suit his purposes.
    (Pause.)
We're certainly not going to claim he did this for your benefit.
That makes you look involved.

JENNIFER
But why would he? Mark's not a killer, he's a doctor.

RUSSO
Not a doctor — a plastic surgeon. Someone consumed by the su-
perficial.

JENNIFER
But he's not, and he wouldn't.

RUSSO

No? Then who would? We know somebody did — unless you really did murder Christine Lowery.

JENNIFER

I didn't.

RUSSO

Fine. Then whoever did, framed you. Who? Any other candidates? Ever read any Sherlock Holmes? "When you have eliminated the impossible, whatever remains, however improbable, must be the truth." Well, we've eliminated the impossible, everything except that Dr. Mark Lowery framed you for the murder of his wife. So, however improbable that is to you — it's true.

(The lights fade on RUSSO's office, and come up on RUSSO and the PROSECUTOR standing in the FRONT AREA, in court.)

RUSSO

Your Honor, it is critical to our case that we be permitted to introduce evidence establishing Mark Lowery's motive to kill his wife — and frame Jennifer Creighton in his place.

PROSECUTOR

Dr. Lowery is not on trial here.

RUSSO

He should be.

(The lights fade on RUSSO and the PROSECUTOR.)

VOICE of JUDGE

I'm denying your application.

(Spotlight on OLIVETTI standing at the right of the FRONT AREA. He is reading from the DIARY.)

OLIVETTI

No one ever got anywhere being weak. Appearing to be weak is another matter entirely. Men need to be needed.

*(RUSSO's office.   JENNIFER stands as RUSSO opens an
envelope with his gold-plated letter opener.)*

RUSSO

We just got this list of the prosecution's witnesses.
        (He reads.)
Who is Randall Dunn?

(There is a pause.)

JENNIFER

He's the man who sold me my gun.

RUSSO

        (Thinks it over.)
So they know about the gun. That's more circumstantial evidence
— but it's still circumstantial.   It doesn't prove it was your gun
that shot Christine Lowery. And certainly doesn't prove that you
pulled the trigger.

JENNIFER

Right.

RUSSO

But it does make it that much more important that we show that
someone else had access to everything the prosecution will be re-
lying on: your scarf, your shoes. Everything.

JENNIFER

Okay.

RUSSO

Also — why did you buy the gun? Did someone suggest buying
it to you? You see where I'm going?

JENNIFER

I think so.

RUSSO

Did Mark Lowery suggest you buy it?

JENNIFER

Well, he kept telling me about women my age who he'd operated on because they'd been attacked and slashed. He even showed me pictures. I don't react well to seeing a lot of blood. I told him I felt ill. He told me that I needed to protect myself just in case.

RUSSO

That's good.

JENNIFER

But I don't think —

VOICE of SECRETARY
(On the intercom.)
Mr. Russo, your wife's on line one.

RUSSO
(To JENNIFER.)
Sorry.
(He picks up the phone.)
Thank you, Stephanie.
(Pushes button.)
Diane, you really can't keep interrupting me when I'm in a meeting. What is it now?

(Spotlight on DIANE RUSSO standing in the FRONT AREA, holding a telephone receiver.)

DIANE

The cable is out.

RUSSO

What am I supposed to do about it?

DIANE

Can't you call the company?

RUSSO

I really can't. Maybe Helen can help you. Please try to handle this yourself. Sorry.
(He hangs up. The light fades on DIANE.)

She's really got to learn to be a little more independent. I'm sorry.
Where were we?

JENNIFER

You were trying to convince me that Mark tricked me into buying
a gun.

RUSSO

To put it plainly, yes.

JENNIFER

I really can't believe that Mark was doing that. He was worried
about me.

RUSSO

Jennifer, if Mark Lowery hadn't shown you those pictures, would
you ever have considered buying a gun?

JENNIFER

No, but —

RUSSO

But nothing. Mark Lowery had to be behind this.

JENNIFER

It's just not possible.

RUSSO

No, then if not Mark, who? You tell me.
        (JENNIFER doesn't answer.)
Then it was Mark. It had to be. Accept it. Remember Sherlock
Holmes: "Whatever remains, however improbable, must be the
truth."

JENNIFER
(Indicating the picture on RUSSO's desk.)
Is that your wife?

RUSSO

Many years ago. Her happy years.
        (Pause.)

She's been struggling with depression for a long time now.

JENNIFER

That's too bad. I'm sorry.

RUSSO

It's often a challenge.

JENNIFER

I could tell.

RUSSO

A lot of people have it a lot worse.

JENNIFER

I suppose.

(The lights fade on RUSSO's office and come up on DIANE standing in the FRONT AREA as RUSSO enters.)

DIANE

What's your hurry?

RUSSO

I have to be in court by nine-thirty.

DIANE

That never made you rush before. Then again, you never represented Little Miss Pouty Lips before.

RUSSO

Stop it, Diane. You sound like an idiot.

DIANE

Watch it, Tom. She's got manipulative killer bitch written all over her. Don't get involved.

RUSSO

She's a case, Diane. A tool. A theatrical prop in my performance.
        (Pause.)
Where's Helen?

                              DIANE
She's not feeling well. I gave her one of my pills.

                              RUSSO
Brilliant. Also illegal.

                              DIANE
I thought you were in a hurry.

                              RUSSO
I am. Good-bye.

                              DIANE
Manipulative killer bitch. Remember.

                              RUSSO
Fortunately, she only kills the wives, not the husbands.

          (*As the lights fade, a spotlight shines on OLIVETTI standing
          at the right of the FRONT AREA. He is reading from the
          DIARY.*)

                             OLIVETTI
Can I trust him? Has he ever meant what he says? Does he mean
it now?

          (*The lights come up on RUSSO standing in the FRONT
          AREA, in court.*)

                              RUSSO
Ladies and gentlemen of the jury, if you found *my* wallet on the
floor of *your* house, your first reaction probably would be: "Hey,
Russo, what were you doing in my house?" But let's say you then
found out that someone else in *your* house had been spending a
lot of time in mine. And let's also say you found out that this person needed money and had once been arrested for shoplifting.
That would make you reconsider your initial suspicion that I'd
ever been in your house, wouldn't it? Well, as this trial progress-
es, ladies and gentlemen, you are going to hear a lot of facts that
are going to make you reconsider who really shot and killed
Christine Lowery, and why any evidence exists connecting Jen-

nifer Creighton to this case.

> *(The lights fade and come up on RUSSO's office. MURPHY sits facing RUSSO, behind his desk.)*

MURPHY

When are you going to ask her where the gun is?

RUSSO

When I'm sure of the answer I want.

MURPHY

I still can't figure out why you're doing this. Is Creighton's money that important to you?

RUSSO

I love a challenge. Winning doesn't mean much if you don't take tough cases.

MURPHY

We're all smoke and mirrors on this one, Tom, and you know it.

RUSSO

I don't mind smoke.
> *(Preening.)*
And I love mirrors.

VOICE of SECRETARY
> *(On the intercom.)*
You wife's on the phone. She sounds different, sick.
> *(RUSSO picks up the phone.)*

VOICE
> *(Tearful.)*
Tommy? It's me.

RUSSO

Look, I can't talk now.

VOICE

When, then, Tommy?

                              RUSSO
Later.

                              VOICE
It's always "later."

                              RUSSO
Please stop this.

                              VOICE
I can't, Tommy, I can't.

                              RUSSO
Are you alone?

                              VOICE
Why are you asking that?

                              RUSSO
Because you're usually not alone. Is there anyone there with you?

                              VOICE
No.

                              RUSSO
You really have to get control of yourself. This is getting out of
hand.

                              VOICE
We have to talk, Tommy.

                              RUSSO
But not when I'm working. We'll deal with this later. Good-bye.
          (He hangs up. To MURPHY.)
You know, she started asking me about Diane.

                              MURPHY
Who?

                              RUSSO
Jennifer Creighton. She started getting very personal. Crossing

the line.

MURPHY

She's just like that. Touchy-feely. I wouldn't think twice about it.

RUSSO

She's starting to give me the creeps.

(The lights fade on RUSSO's office as a spotlight shines on OLIVETTI standing at the right of the FRONT AREA. He is reading from the DIARY.)

OLIVETTI

I'd do anything for him, if only he'd stay with me. But nothing is working out as we planned. As he promised.

(The lights rise again on RUSSO's office. RUSSO and JEN-NIFER are present. She is holding a cardboard carton.)

JENNIFER

I'm very grateful for all that you're doing for me, Mr. Russo.

RUSSO

You really shouldn't have. Your father is paying me very gener-ously.

JENNIFER

Well, I saw this — and I just had to buy it for you.

(She hands him the box. He places it on the desk, slits open the top with his gold-plated letter opener, and looks inside.)

RUSSO

What is it?

JENNIFER

Dig inside.

RUSSO

(Half-jokingly.)

You dig inside.

(JENNIFER does, taking out styrofoam pieces, and then a small statue.)

JENNIFER

It's Sherlock Holmes. Since you quote him all the time.

RUSSO

It's very nice. Thank you.

JENNIFER

You're very welcome. It's the least I could do.

RUSSO

In fact, that belongs on my mantelpiece at home.

JENNIFER

I'm flattered. A place of honor.

RUSSO

Do you think you could repack it in the box for me, just the way it was? I always wind up with pieces left over.

JENNIFER

Sure.
    (As she does.)
How is your wife doing?

(The lights fade on RUSSO's office, and a spotlight shines on MARK LOWERY, sitting in a witness chair to the left in the FRONT AREA.)

LOWERY

I told Jennifer to meet me at the Wagon Wheel Restaurant at seven o'clock. I arrived a few minutes before seven. Jennifer wasn't there. I asked for a booth, preferably in the back. I really didn't want people seeing us together. They sat me in a booth and I just waited. At about seven-fifteen, Jennifer called me on her cell-phone to say she would be late. She didn't appear until about seven-thirty. She seemed out of breath. Excited. Distracted.

(Another spotlight comes up on RUSSO, standing in the

FRONT AREA facing LOWERY.)

RUSSO

Dr. Lowery, did you ever discuss with Ms. Creighton her safety?

LOWERY

I don't know what you mean.

RUSSO

Did you ever suggest to her that she was in danger from muggers, slashers, people like that?

LOWERY

We talked about a lot of things. It may have come up.

RUSSO

Didn't you do much more than talk about this subject?   Didn't you, in fact, show Ms. Creighton numerous pictures you have of patients you've treated because they'd been slashed in the face by an attacker, and warn her that, without proper protection, she might be victimized in this manner?

LOWERY

I don't recall that.

RUSSO

Have you treated people like that in your practice?

LOWERY

Every cosmetic surgeon repairs facial lacerations.

RUSSO

Do you keep pictures of these patients, showing their appearance before their surgery?

LOWERY

These patients are photographed, yes.

RUSSO

But you never showed these photographs to Ms. Creighton? Do you think it was just a lucky guess that she knew you had them?

LOWERY

I said I didn't remember showing them to her.

RUSSO

But you may have?

LOWERY

I may have.

RUSSO

And you may have mentioned that she needed extra protection?

LOWERY

I suppose I could have.

RUSSO

Let me ask you something else, Dr. Lowery. Have you ever been to Ms. Creighton's apartment?

LOWERY

Yes.

RUSSO

With her, or without her?

LOWERY

Always with her.

RUSSO

Never without her?

LOWERY

Never.

RUSSO

Ever get there with her, and find you couldn't get in?

LOWERY

I think there was one time, yes. Jennifer had left her keys inside.

RUSSO

Did you get in?

LOWERY

Yes, I think we did.

RUSSO

How?   Did you call a locksmith, or are you handy with a credit card?

LOWERY

No. I believe she had a spare key.

RUSSO

In her purse?

LOWERY

No, I believe it was hidden in the laundry room.

RUSSO

Thank you.

(The spotlight shifts from LOWERY and RUSSO to OLIVETTI standing at the right of the FRONT AREA.   He is reading from the DIARY.)

OLIVETTI

He notices everything.   He remembers everything.   He has to. Otherwise, he couldn't keep his lies straight.

(The spotlight fades on OLIVETTI. There is a momentary pause.)

VOICE of JUDGE

Detective Olivetti, you may proceed.

(Another spotlight shines on OLIVETTI, now sitting in a witness chair in the center of the FRONT AREA.)

OLIVETTI

Thank you, Your Honor.

(Pause.)
We obtained the cellphone records for Ms. Creighton's cellphone. At seven-seventeen p.m. on the night in question, Ms. Creighton made a call to the cellphone of Dr. Mark Lowery. We know that the call was answered by Dr. Lowery. If it had gone to his voicemail, it would have been answered at his provider's central station. This call was answered at his actual cellphone. The call lasted twenty-three seconds. We can determine the location of the sender and recipient by determining which cell towers processed the call. They show that Ms. Creighton placed this call in the proximity of the Lowery home. The call reached Dr. Lowery through the cell tower that serves the Wagon Wheel Restaurant.

> *(The lights fade on OLIVETTI and come up on RUSSO's office. RUSSO and JENNIFER are talking.)*

JENNIFER

Why would I call him to say I'd be late? I didn't think I was late. I thought I was on time.

RUSSO

Did you have your cellphone with you?

JENNIFER

Why do you keep asking me these questions? I don't constantly inventory my pocketbook.

RUSSO

(A little louder.)
This is critical information.

JENNIFER

Please don't yell at me. I thought you liked me.

RUSSO

I do like you, Jennifer. But the prosecutor doesn't. He won't be holding your hand. So get used to it.

JENNIFER

I don't know if I can testify.

RUSSO

I don't think you have any choice. This whole case comes down to you. You have to convince this jury that Mark Lowery framed you for the murder of his wife. You have to say it, not me. From me, it's just some lawyer talking. If it's not in those exact words, it better be close — and with that sense of absolute certainty. You have to convince this jury just as you convinced Gene and me.

JENNIFER

But I'm not sure.

RUSSO

Then get sure.

JENNIFER

(Quietly.)

Okay.

RUSSO

But, when you testify, the prosecutor is going to ask you about the gun.

JENNIFER

Yeah — thanks to Randy Dunn and his big mouth.

RUSSO

This has nothing to do with Randy Dunn.

JENNIFER

No? If he hadn't snitched to the police —

RUSSO

Jennifer, this case is not about Randall Dunn. You weren't framed by Randall Dunn. You bought the gun because Mark Lowery convinced you to buy the gun, correct?

JENNIFER

Right.

RUSSO

Then that's your message, nothing else. But the prosecutor is then going to ask you where the gun is now. Hear me out before you say anything. If — if, that is, you know where the gun is, you have to tell him, and then he'll get a search warrant and seize it and test it, and if Mark used that gun, it will match the bullets that killed Christine. *If* you know where it is. Do you follow what I'm saying?

JENNIFER

I think so.

RUSSO

So, pretend I'm the prosecutor: "Ms. Creighton, where is this gun now?"

JENNIFER
(With her face in her hands, thinking hard.)
I really don't know. After Mrs. Lowery's death, I looked for it. But it was gone. I haven't seen it since.

RUSSO

If you can do that with your eyes open, we'll be fine.

(The lights fade on RUSSO's office, and a spotlight shines on JENNIFER in a witness chair in the center of the FRONT AREA.)

JENNIFER
No, Mr. Russo, I definitely did not shoot Christine Lowery.
(A change of lighting.)
I arrived at the Wagon Wheel Restaurant at seven-thirty because Mark told me to arrive at seven-thirty.
(A change of lighting.)
No, I have no idea where my scarf or my cellphone were at the time. Mr. Russo, let me tell you something about women's pocketbooks.
(A change of lighting.)
Mark Lowery had access to everything I own. He knew I left a spare key to my apartment hidden in the laundry room of my building. He could have gone in and out of my apartment whenever he wished. I think — I think he framed me.

(Another spotlight comes up on the PROSECUTOR, standing in the FRONT AREA facing JENNIFER.)

PROSECUTOR

Ms. Creighton, do you own a safe deposit box at the First Federal Bank?

JENNFIER

(Nervous.)

Yes.

PROSECUTOR

Two days after Christine Lowery was murdered, did you visit that safe deposit box?
(There is a long pause.)
Perhaps reviewing the bank's record of that visit would refresh your recollection.

JENNIFER

Yes, I did.

PROSECUTOR

What was the purpose of your visit?

JENNIFER

I — I — don't recall.

PROSECUTOR

Well, perhaps I can help you to remember. What things do you keep in your safe deposit box, Ms. Creighton?

JENNIFER

Some papers. Some bonds, mostly.

PROSECUTOR

Did you suddenly need those papers, those bonds?

JENNIFER

I don't recall.

PROSECUTOR

Ms. Creighton, did you purchase a thirty-two caliber revolver from Randall Dunn?

JENNIFER
(More comfortable.)
Yes, I did. Mark Lowery told me that I needed to get —

PROSECUTOR
(Cutting her off.)
You visited your safe deposit box on that occasion to put that revolver in it, didn't you?

JENNIFER

I don't recall.

PROSECUTOR

You don't recall!? Is that something you're likely to forget? Either you did or you didn't — which is it?

JENNIFER
(Flustered.)
Look, I didn't know what to do. I read about Christine. The gun smelled funny. I didn't want to throw it away, because I thought that would make me look like I'd done something wrong. I didn't know what else to do.

(The spotlight fades on JENNIFER.)

PROSECUTOR

Your Honor, we have a court order here which we would ask you to sign, requiring the First Federal Bank to open Ms. Creighton's safe deposit box and permitting us to seize Ms. Creighton's thirty-two caliber revolver.

(The spotlight fades on the PROSECUTOR and comes up on RUSSO and JENNIFER to the far right of the FRONT AREA.)

JENNIFER

I'm sorry, I'm sorry. He didn't ask the questions the way you said he would ask them. I didn't know what else to say.

RUSSO

Don't worry about it. These things happen. What's done is done.

JENNIFER

But what are we going to do?

RUSSO

First, we're going to keep our heads. Second, we're going to remember that the trial isn't over. The trial isn't close to being over. Jennifer, you were only our first witness. And third, we're going to turn your little mistake to our advantage.

JENNIFER

How do we do that?

RUSSO

When I figure that part out, I'll tell you. But don't worry, I always figure that part out. Look, I'll be working from home tonight. Why don't you come over about eight. Write down this address.

(*The spotlight fades. The stage is in darkness. There is the sound of a doorbell. Then there is the sound of knocking and a door opening. A sliver of light comes in. JENNIFER slowly enters the FRONT AREA.*)

JENNIFER

Mr. Russo? Mr. Russo?

(*She steps in something strange and feels for an imaginary light switch. The lights come on in the FRONT AREA. A blonde WOMAN lies on the floor, her face turned away, apparently bludgeoned to death with the Sherlock Holmes statue. JENNIFER looks down and realizes she is standing in blood. She screams, tries to wipe her shoes, turns, and runs off. A spotlight remains on the blonde WOMAN's dead body.*)

VOICE of FIRST TV REPORTER

Neighbors heard a scream shortly after eight o'clock, and saw a woman, meeting Ms. Creighton's description, running from the Russo home.

                    VOICE of SECOND TV REPORTER
          (Overlapping.)
According to police, Jennifer Creighton's fingerprints were found on the entrance of the Russo house and on the murder weapon.

                    VOICE of THIRD TV REPORTER
          (Overlapping.)
Police say Creighton's shoes were soaked with the victim's blood.

          (A spotlight on MURPHY and JENNIFER in the FRONT AREA.)

                    MURPHY
My client maintains her innocence. We have nothing more to say at this time.

                    JENNIFER
          (Stepping in front of MURPHY.)
I've been framed.

                    CURTAIN

                    END OF ACT I

ACT II

(OLIVETTI stands in a spotlight shining on the right of the FRONT AREA. He is flipping through the DIARY. OLIVETTI then reads aloud.)

OLIVETTI

It's as if the fates have conspired against me. Not just the fates. Everything.

(The light fades on OLIVETTI and rises on RUSSO's office. RUSSO sits at his desk, fiddling with his gold-plated letter opener. MURPHY stands quietly.)

MURPHY

I spoke to the judge. He's not happy.

RUSSO

Like I give a fuck. Does he really expect his happiness to be my primary concern?

MURPHY

I don't know what he expects — other than finishing this trial without Christine Lowery's mother and the jury complaining that it's taking too long. Bottom line: he'll let you out of the case, but not me. He'll question the jury about what they've read and heard, but assuming the trial can continue, he said he'll only grant us a one-week adjournment, no more.

RUSSO

I really don't care.
(Pause.)
This is all your fault, you know.

MURPHY

My fault?

                         RUSSO
Yes, your fault.

                         MURPHY
How is it my fault?

                         RUSSO
You brought me the case.

                         MURPHY
I came to you for advice about *my* case. You're the one who insisted on taking over.

                         RUSSO
You wanted me to take over.

                         MURPHY
No, I didn't.   The minute you saw all the press coverage, you
couldn't resist. Like a moth to a flame.

                         RUSSO
You dared me.

                         MURPHY
How's that again?

                         RUSSO
You said the case was unwinnable.

          (*They pause.*)

                         MURPHY
By the way, the police found the gun. It matches the bullets taken
from Christine Lowery's body. Jennifer's fingerprints are all over
it. Mark Lowery's prints are nowhere to be found. Here —
          (*Reaching into his briefcase.*)
Here's a copy of the report.

                         RUSSO
          (*Not bothering to look.*)
Big surprise.

MURPHY

So not only am I stuck on this case, I'm stuck with a defense I can't pull off. And it's way past the point of no return. We're the fucking Charge of the Light Brigade. Into the valley of death we ride. It's frame-up or die.

RUSSO

Then switch to a psychiatric defense if you feel that way.

MURPHY

Now you're okay with a psychiatric defense?

RUSSO

Now there's new evidence that she's crazy.

MURPHY

(After a pause.)
Just so you know, she says *you* did it.

RUSSO

Sure she does. Just like she says Mark Lowery killed his wife.

MURPHY

Says so. But doesn't think so — or at least she didn't. Not at first, anyway. Not like this. Not until we convinced her that he must have. And even then, she didn't want to believe it. But about this one, she has no doubts, no hesitation. This time's different.

RUSSO

And does she explain why?

MURPHY

Apparently, you told her that Diane is a manic-depressive, that she can't do anything on her own, that she never leaves the house.

RUSSO

Of course, she leaves the house. Obviously — she left the house.

MURPHY

That she's become too much of a burden on you.

VOICE of SECRETARY
(On the intercom.)
Mr. Russo, your wife is here to see you.

RUSSO
(Picks up phone.)
I'll be right out.
(To MURPHY.)
I guess Jennifer conveniently omitted the minor fact that NO ONE
KILLED DIANE!   That DIANE WASN'T HOME!   That DIANE
WAS OUT WITH ME!
(Pause.)
Does she explain why someone KILLED DIANE'S SISTER!?

MURPHY
No.

RUSSO
You're damn right, no.

MURPHY
She doesn't know.

RUSSO
Well, *I* know. Helen was killed by someone who only knew Diane
from an old picture —
(Holds up framed photograph on his desk.)
— who couldn't tell the difference.
(Walks toward the "door.")
Or does she think I couldn't tell the difference either?
(Exits.)

MURPHY
No, she doesn't.

(RUSSO returns with DIANE. MURPHY goes to her.)

MURPHY
Hi, Diane.
(Hugs her.)

DIANE

Hi, Gene.

MURPHY

My condolences.

DIANE

Thanks.

MURPHY

I'm pleasantly surprised to see you here.

DIANE

I had to get out of that house.

MURPHY

Glad to see that you're well enough to drive.

DIANE

I took a taxi.
> *(Pause.)*

I'm thinking of selling it. The house. I can't stay there alone. Certainly not any more.

MURPHY

> *(To RUSSO.)*

Really?

RUSSO

It's Diane's decision.

DIANE

Of course it is, Tom. It's my house.

RUSSO

> *(To MURPHY.)*

A gift from Daddy.

DIANE

Don't mock my father's generosity.
> *(Looking around.)*

It's amazing how successful you can become when you look successful.

MURPHY
(Uncomfortable.)
Hey, I better go. I've got a lot to do to get ready for next week.

DIANE
You're not going to continue to defend that woman, are you, Gene?

MURPHY
I've got no choice. We're in the middle of a trial and the judge won't let me off the case. Well, bye now. It's really nice to see you out and about, Diane.

DIANE
Thanks.

(MURPHY goes.)

DIANE
I like him.

RUSSO
He's a good man.

DIANE
Why he hangs out with you, I'll never know.

RUSSO
I give him fashion tips.

DIANE
I had an interesting talk with the taxi driver on the way over here. Tom, what was your relationship with Jennifer Creighton?

RUSSO
How many times do we have to do this? You know the answer.

DIANE

I want to hear it again.

RUSSO

She was my client.

DIANE

Was that all?

RUSSO

That was all.

DIANE

Everybody seems to think she killed Helen — in other words, tried to kill me — for the same reason she killed Christine Lowery. Which only makes sense if her relationship with you was the same as her relationship with Mark Lowery.

RUSSO

It wasn't.

DIANE

I know there've been other women. I'm not an idiot, and I know I've been difficult to live with. I looked the other way as long as it wasn't shoved under my nose. You're you. A pompous prick, who needs to have someone fawn over you. And I haven't the stomach for it. I know why you stay with me. But I *warned* you about this one. I could see it in her eyes. How could you be so reckless to get involved with someone who kills her lovers' wives?

RUSSO

Stop listening to cab drivers. You're all acting like Jennifer Creighton was a rational person. She grew up neglected by a father who was too busy making money. Mark Lowery paid attention to her. So she fixated on him, obsessed over him, tried to possess him. I paid attention to her. I tried to help her. It was my job. That's the only thing we have in common.

DIANE

You know the worst part about your lying? That you're so good at it.

RUSSO
You're right about one thing.

DIANE
What?

RUSSO
I should have seen the signs.   The questions about my personal
life — about my relationship with you.   I talked to Gene about it,
but didn't do anything else — take any precautions.

DIANE
What did you tell her about me?

RUSSO
Nothing of any importance.

DIANE
That I'm an emotional cripple who survives on anti-depressants?
                    (RUSSO doesn't respond.)
Did you tell her about our marriage?   How about our finances?

RUSSO
No. Why would I ever tell a client — ?

DIANE
Why didn't you tell her that I've got all the money, and that you
can't get your hands on it, no matter what?   No, I bet you didn't
tell her that little piece of information.

> *(The light fades on RUSSO's office. Spotlight on OLIVETTI
> standing at the right of the FRONT AREA.   He is reading
> from the DIARY.)*

OLIVETTI
I used to know just what string to pull. Now I'm not so sure.

> *(Spotlight on MURPHY and the PROSECUTOR in the
> FRONT AREA.)*

MURPHY

Your Honor, I appreciate that we're in the middle of a murder trial, that Christine Lowery's family is under an enormous strain, and that twelve jurors have put their lives on hold to serve their community and want to finish their civic duty.   But there is no way *any* case can continue under these circumstances.   Ms. Creighton is still presumed innocent of the murder of Christine Lowery. She can't get a fair trial with all the publicity surrounding the murder of Mr. Russo's sister-in-law. Ms. Creighton hasn't even been charged with this second crime, but the media has all but convicted her. The court should declare a mistrial, let some time pass, and then start fresh.

PROSECUTOR

The defense's request has nothing to do with getting a fair trial, Your Honor. Just the opposite, the defense wants to turn this new crime to its tactical advantage. It's tested its "I was framed" defense before this jury, seen it reduced to tatters, and now wants to "start fresh," as Mr. Murphy puts it, with a new jury — to test something radically different. The defense is trying to play games with the truth, and the court should not permit it. In fact, I think *I* should be allowed to show this jury that every time the defendant is linked to a homicide scene, she cries, "Frame-up."

(*The light fades on MURPHY and the PROSECUTOR in the FRONT AREA.*)

VOICE of JUDGE

I am denying both of your applications, counselors. No evidence of this new crime will be permitted at this trial — but this trial is going forward. I've questioned each juror, Mr. Murphy. Each one has promised me that he or she will judge this case on the evidence alone. You have one week to get ready to continue the defense.

(*The lights come up on RUSSO's office.   RUSSO is behind his desk. OLIVETTI enters.*)

OLIVETTI

I hope I'm not disturbing you.

                         RUSSO

Not at all, Detective.

                        OLIVETTI

I'm surprised to see you back at work. You really should take
some time off. Take your wife fishing. It clears the head.

                         RUSSO

I might do that.

                        OLIVETTI

But as long as you're here, do you have a few minutes for me?

                         RUSSO

However I can help.

                        OLIVETTI

I really appreciate this.
            (Pause.)
How long had your sister-in-law been staying with you?

                         RUSSO

A few weeks.

                        OLIVETTI

Why was that?

                         RUSSO

I don't like leaving my wife alone. Our housekeeper's daughter
was having a baby. So Diane asked Helen to stay with us until
Marianela returned.

                        OLIVETTI

Were your wife and her sister close?

                         RUSSO

In some ways. Helen was only two years younger, so that made
them close. They looked a lot alike, as everybody now knows.
But their personalities were polar opposites. Must have something to do with birth order. The oldest is more serious, the
youngest more frivolous. Diane has a dark view of the world,

which certainly doesn't help you battle depression.   Not Helen.
No, she assumed everything would always turn out fine, that she
could get whatever she wanted.

OLIVETTI

Mr. Murphy won't let us speak to Ms. Creighton.

RUSSO

That can't surprise you.

OLIVETTI

Not really. So the only thing we know she's said is that — she'd
been framed.

RUSSO

That sounds familiar.

OLIVETTI

I thought of that, too. The girl who cried, "Framed." Like the boy
who cried, "Wolf." Same idea. No one pays attention to you the
second time if you lied about the wolf the first time. That about
right?

RUSSO

Something like that.

OLIVETTI

But what if you only cried, "Wolf," the first time because someone
told you he'd actually seen a wolf and said you better tell people
about it?   Then the second time doesn't seem so unbelievable,
does it?

RUSSO

Now who's fishing, Detective?

*(The lights fade on RUSSO's office. Spotlight on OLIVETTI
standing at the right of the FRONT AREA.   He is reading
from the DIARY.)*

OLIVETTI

I don't know where my mind stops and his begins. He's in my head all the time. I want to yell, "Stop!" Everything's a blur. It's too exhausting.

> *(The lights rise on RUSSO's office. RUSSO and MURPHY are present. MURPHY puts a cellphone down on the table opposite RUSSO's desk.)*

MURPHY

Call my cellphone.

RUSSO

I don't get it.

MURPHY

Just call my cellphone.

> *(RUSSO picks up his phone and dials. MURPHY's cellphone on the table rings, and then stops.)*

MURPHY

What do you hear?

RUSSO

I hear you.

MURPHY

How do you mean? From across the room — or over the phone?

RUSSO

Over the phone. I hear you talking through the phone.

MURPHY

Exactly.

RUSSO

I don't get it.

MURPHY

Ever look down the list of settings on your phone?

RUSSO

No.

MURPHY

Of course not. No one does. But it's there: auto answer. You can set the phone to answer calls automatically. After one ring, two rings, whatever you want. Just like you had answered it yourself.

RUSSO

And this means that the blood on Jennifer Creighton's clothing was not Christine Lowery's?

MURPHY

No, but it means that Mark Lowery didn't have to be at the Wagon Wheel Restaurant in order for his cellphone to receive a call at the Wagon Wheel Restaurant. His cellphone could have done it all by itself.

(Lights fade in RUSSO's office, and a spotlight comes up on OLIVETTI, seated in a chair in the FRONT AREA.)

OLIVETTI

We seized Ms. Creighton's thirty-two caliber revolver from her safe deposit box. It had been fully loaded with five cartridges. Two had been fired. Three were unfired. We emptied the three loaded cartridges and two spent shell casings. We checked the revolver for fingerprints. There were numerous prints belonging to Jennifer Creighton on the gun. We found no one else's prints anywhere.

(Spotlight on MURPHY standing in the FRONT AREA.)

MURPHY

Detective, I've read your ballistics and fingerprint reports, and you make it sound as if fingerprints were only on the gun itself.

OLIVETTI

That's correct.

MURPHY

No prints on the cartridges?

> OLIVETTI

No, sir.

> MURPHY

How about the spent shells?

> OLIVETTI

No, sir.

> MURPHY

No partial prints, no smudges.

> OLIVETTI

Not that we found.

> MURPHY

Well, could you have missed them?

> OLIVETTI

That's highly unlikely.

> MURPHY

That's impossible, wouldn't you agree?

> OLIVETTI

Yes, sir.

> MURPHY

How can this be? Wouldn't the act of loading a revolver normally leave prints on the bullets?

> OLIVETTI

Not if you were careful not to leave prints.

> MURPHY

But you would concede, Detective, would you not, that Jennifer Creighton was not careful about *not* leaving prints on this gun.

> OLIVETTI

She did leave a lot of prints, yes.

MURPHY

So if, as you say, the person who loaded this gun was careful not to leave prints, then doesn't it follow that the person who loaded this gun was *not* Jennifer Creighton?

(OLIVETTI thinks, as the spotlight on him fades.)

MURPHY

Your Honor, according to previous testimony, police obtained all of their information about the alleged Creighton-Lowery seven-seventeen p.m. call from Jennifer Creighton's cellphone records, not from Mark Lowery's phone records. I would like to introduce Dr. Lowery's records, subject to connection.

(Holds up some papers.)

They show that, right after Mark Lowery's cellphone received the twenty-three-second call from Jennifer Creighton's cellphone, purportedly while he was at the Wagon Wheel Restaurant, Mark Lowery's phone received three other calls, all from the same number. One at seven-twenty-two p.m. lasting twelve seconds, one a minute later lasting eight seconds, and one a minute after that lasting twenty-six seconds. All from the number 413-555-6538. That number is listed to Terry Sanderson. Ms. Sanderson is the neighbor who found Christine Lowery's body.

(The spotlight fades on MURPHY, and comes up on TERRY SANDERSON, in the witness chair.)

SANDERSON

After I called nine-one-one, I tried to call Mark. All I got was the sound of people talking, dishes clattering — like in a restaurant. But Mark never said anything. I tried three times, but nothing.

(The spotlight fades on SANDERSON, and comes up on MURPHY standing in the FRONT AREA.)

MURPHY

Ladies and gentlemen of the jury, Mark Lowery wasn't in the Wagon Wheel between seven and seven-thirty that night. His phone was — set to automatically answer any calls, probably with the ringer turned off. But Mark wasn't. He told Jennifer to meet him at seven-thirty. He got there at seven, got an out-of-the-way

booth in a dark corner. He told the waitress he wouldn't be ordering anything until Jennifer arrived so she wouldn't pay attention
to him for a while. Then he put his "auto answer" cellphone under the seat or under a napkin and left. He took Jennifer's gun,
which he loaded and handled wearing gloves, along with her
shoe, her scarf, and her cellphone — all collected secretly from her
apartment at various times. Lowery then went to his house, killed
his wife, let some blood splatter, shook out some fibers, and made
a call to himself on Jennifer's cellphone — to make it appear that
he was at the restaurant, talking on his phone, when the murder
took place. He did this to cinch his alibi and tighten the noose
even further around Jennifer Creighton's neck. Then he hurried
back to the Wagon Wheel. There was only one thing he didn't
foresee: that Terry Sanderson, a concerned neighbor, would call
him *three times* while his phone was hidden under his restaurant
seat. Mark Lowery didn't foresee Terry Sanderson uncovering the
fact that, while Dr. Lowery's phone was at the restaurant answer-
ing her calls, Mark Lowery was not.

(RUSSO's office, with RUSSO and OLIVETTI present.)

OLIVETTI
Remember, on my last visit, we discussed the the boy who cried,
"Wolf"? Maybe the boy cried, "Wolf," the first time because there
really was a wolf.

RUSSO
Detective, you're confusing an acquittal with innocence. Do I really have to tell *you* what I tell the press anytime someone in America is found "not guilty"?

OLIVETTI
I know the difference. But Mr. Murphy did make a very convincing case.

RUSSO
Gene Murphy did a masterful job of creating a reasonable doubt
in the minds of the jurors. *That's* why Jennifer Creighton was acquitted.

OLIVETTI

Actually, he gave *you* the credit for designing the defense strategy. He says that, at first, he thought no jury would buy it. But you insisted. And because you did, he says, he was forced to hunt down the evidence that acquitted her — the phone records and so forth. Things he'd've missed if you hadn't gotten involved. If you hadn't insisted on this defense and committed him to it.

RUSSO

He gives me too much credit.

OLIVETTI

Or hadn't insisted on taking this case — over his objections, or so he claims.

RUSSO
(A touch too dramatically.)
Then shame on me. There was no evidence linking Mark Lowery to this crime. Just gaps in the evidence, just small openings we pried a little wider and exploited. We didn't stop for a minute and consider that this was a man whose wife had been murdered, before we pointed fingers at him.
(Using his gold-plated letter opener as the pointer.)
I see things from his perspective a little better now. Mark Lowery is a victim. A victim — and shame on all of us.

OLIVETTI

So I guess this means you don't think he framed her anymore?

RUSSO

I'm not her lawyer anymore.

(OLIVETTI turns to go, then stops.)

OLIVETTI

But suddenly it sounds so important to you that Jennifer Creighton really did murder Christine Lowery. That's not like you, Mr. Russo. You always maintain your client's innocence to the very last, and with such certainty, too. I think it's one secret of your success. And after an acquittal, I'd imagine that proclaiming her innocence would be a fairly easy thing to keep up. But you're doing just the opposite. It's not like you.

> *(The lights fade on RUSSO's office and come up on DIANE standing in the FRONT AREA as OLIVETTI enters. To the right are two suitcases, one closed and standing, the other lying flat and open. A pile of women's clothes are next to the open suitcase.)*

OLIVETTI

Mrs. Russo, thanks very much for speaking with me.

DIANE

I've been packing my sister's things. Do you mind if I continue while we talk?

OLIVETTI

Not at all.

> *(DIANE sits next to the open suitcase and begins folding clothes and laying them neatly in the suitcase.)*

DIANE

I hope you do a better job with Jennifer Creighton this time, Detective.

OLIVETTI

Frankly, I don't know.

DIANE

What does that mean?

OLIVETTI

It means —
> *(Pause.)*
Perhaps you could tell me a little more about your sister.

DIANE
> *(As she folds.)*
My sister was outgoing, full of life. Everybody loved her.

OLIVETTI

Not everybody, it seems.

DIANE

No, everybody. What happened to her was meant for me.

OLIVETTI

Maybe.
(Pause.)
Did you notice anything different about her recently?

DIANE

She was a little down. Slept late. Less talkative. Kept to herself
more. If I didn't know her better, I'd say she was depressed. But I
did know her better — and I know depression. She was a little
moody, that's all.

OLIVETTI

How did she get along with your husband?

DIANE

Helen and Tom? They got along famously. She called him "Tommy," actually. The only one who did. The only one he let call him
"Tommy." But, then again, most men let Helen do whatever she
wanted to do.

OLIVETTI

(After a beat.)
Does your husband have any reason to be afraid of *you*?

DIANE

(She stops folding and looks at OLIVETTI.)
What does that have to do with Jennifer Creighton killing Helen?

OLIVETTI

Perhaps you should let me be the judge of that. Does he? Have a
reason to fear you?

DIANE

(Thinks.)
I do control all his money.

OLIVETTI

That's a provocative statement.

DIANE

(Resumes folding.)

My father didn't trust Tom much.   When we met, Tom was a young, struggling lawyer.   Didn't have a pot to piss in.   Gene Murphy actually became Tom's mentor.   Gene was a couple of years older.   He showed Tom around the courthouse, introduced him to the people he needed to know, showed him how to file papers — all the stuff they didn't teach in law school.

(Pause.)

So my father made a deal with Tom. He'd set him up in a nice office with all the trimmings, except Tom wouldn't own a thing. I would. Tom would lease the office from me, lease the furniture from me, lease the paper clips from me. Everything comes back to me. Tom can't get at it whether I'm dead or alive.

(Pause.)

My father considered it insurance.

OLIVETTI

You see, if Mr. Russo has reason to fear you, he also has a reason to silence anyone who might reveal something to you. Something you wouldn't want to hear.

DIANE

Who? Helen? That's ridiculous.

OLIVETTI

Mrs. Russo, I have a theory. I don't know if you're going to like it. But I think you ought to hear it.

DIANE

I'm listening.

OLIVETTI

Perhaps your sister wasn't killed by mistake. Perhaps your sister was killed under circumstances intended to make it look like a mistake.

                    DIANE
        (After a beat.)
I'm still listening.

                    OLIVETTI
Let's assume Jennifer Creighton is not a murderer. Never was a
murderer. Didn't kill Christine Lowery. Never had any reason to
try to kill you. Let's assume all of that.

                    DIANE
I'm not ready to do that.

                    OLIVETTI
Hear me out. But we know she was here on the night Helen was
murdered. That's for certain. Why was she?

                    DIANE
If it wasn't to kill me, you mean?

                    OLIVETTI
Right. It could only be for one reason. Someone gave her this address. And that someone could only have been your husband.

                    DIANE
        (Stops folding.)
Speaking of provocative statements.

                    OLIVETTI
What did Mr. Russo have to gain by Helen's death?

                    DIANE
Not a thing.

                    OLIVETTI
Was she a threat to him in any way? Was she threatening to reveal
something she knew?

                    DIANE
I would have seen something like that.

OLIVETTI

Because if that were the case, then all the rest begins to make sense.

DIANE

What "rest"?

OLIVETTI

Did you know that Eugene Murphy never wanted your husband to represent Jennifer Creighton.

DIANE

That's only natural.   It was a big case, lots of publicity.   Gene wanted it for himself.

OLIVETTI

There was more to it than that.   Murphy considered the case unwinnable, something your husband wasn't suited for.   But your husband insisted on taking it — and insisted on raising only one defense: that Jennifer had been framed.   Now why?

DIANE

Maybe it was all he had.

OLIVETTI

If that were the case — if this defense was a desperation "Hail, Mary" play — then why take the case at all?   Let Murphy handle it.   It was his case anyway.

DIANE

Okay, maybe he thought it was true.   Maybe even because it *was* true.

OLIVETTI

No.   He doesn't even believe it's true *now*.

DIANE

How can you tell what Tom really believes about anything?

OLIVETTI

I think your husband only took Jennifer Creighton's case so he could convince her to say she'd been framed by Mark Lowery. So that the next time, when she *was* framed, no one would believe her.

DIANE

Framed? By whom?
>(A beat.)
By Tom?

OLIVETTI

Yes.
>(Pause.)
It fits just about everything. Why did Jennifer take the stand, for example — with the gun still missing? Your husband had to know she'd be asked where it was — that she'd be crucified over it. Why put her on the stand under those circumstances?

DIANE

I'm not a lawyer.

OLIVETTI

Neither am I, but I've been around long enough. You just wouldn't. Except if it were real important to you that Jennifer say she'd been framed — by Christine's *husband*, no less — straight from her own lips. Not just some lawyer's argument, but her own statement.

DIANE

This is a lot for me to process.

OLIVETTI

And he couldn't set her up for your sister's murder until after she'd said it. That left a very small window between her testimony and the end of the case — when, presumably, she'd be locked up and no good to him as a patsy.

DIANE

Only if she were convicted.

OLIVETTI

As he expected. As he wanted.

DIANE

So you say.

OLIVETTI

Your husband pushed Jennifer way out on a limb with this "I was framed" defense and then did nothing to prove it. The self-answering cellphone, the clean cartridges, Terry Sanderson's phone calls? Those were all Murphy's doing, after your husband was off the case. Don't get me wrong, Gene Murphy is a good lawyer — but he's no Tom Russo. Whatever Murphy did, your husband could have done — if he wanted to. But he never did.

DIANE

Tom doesn't lose. And certainly not on purpose. He hates the idea of losing.

OLIVETTI

Not this time. Thomas Russo wanted Jennifer Creighton to be convicted of the murder of Christine Lowery. I think he still does. At least, he keeps talking like he wants people to believe that, acquitted or not, Jennifer is guilty.

DIANE

That's because of Helen.

OLIVETTI

I wouldn't be so sure. He wanted that first "I was framed" to be a lie. So the second one would be completely unbelievable. That's why Gene's argument that Jennifer's case was unwinnable made no difference to him. He *wanted* to lose it.

(DIANE looks away.)

OLIVETTI

What?

DIANE

I think Tom told her personal things about me.

OLIVETTI

In the hope she would repeat them, no doubt. Just like the things she'd said about Christine Lowery. He made sure to tell Murphy that Jennifer was asking prying questions about the both of you.

DIANE

Stop listening to cab drivers.

OLIVETTI

Excuse me?

DIANE

Shortly after Helen was killed, I took a taxi ride and the driver kept saying that Jennifer Creighton must have had the same relationship with Tom that she'd had with Mark Lowery. And when I repeated this to Tom, he told me to stop listening to cab drivers.

OLIVETTI

It was all part of the illusion. Jennifer Creighton, the serial wife-killer who always blames the husband.

DIANE

And I thought he was actually having an affair with her.

OLIVETTI

Then all he had to do was kill Helen and lure Jennifer here to be seen, to leave prints, to step in blood. To take the rap. The one thing he didn't count on was Gene Murphy's ability to get her off.

DIANE

That's Tom's ego. If he can't win a case, no one can.
         (Pause.)
But why? Why Helen?

OLIVETTI

It's the one missing piece. It's where I thought you could help. Some reason why it was important for him to silence your sister — or simply to get her out of the way.

DIANE

Such as?

OLIVETTI

She knew something, something that would hurt him. Something she threatened to tell. Tell you, perhaps. An affair, a child — anything that he would regard as too dangerous to risk letting out or you knowing about.

DIANE

They were close. And Helen was a very warm person. But she would never do anything like that to me.

OLIVETTI

Not ordinarily, I'm sure. But people can do things they wouldn't do ordinarily.

DIANE

It couldn't be. We had no secrets.

OLIVETTI

Yes. My point exactly. It was only a matter of time before she told you, and Tom knew it.

DIANE

Told me what!? You don't know anything! You're just guessing!

OLIVETTI

That's true. That's why it's the missing piece. I figured, since you knew her longer and better than anyone else —

DIANE

There was a lot about my sister I never understood.

OLIVETTI

— maybe there was something you knew that might give us an answer.

DIANE

Like what?

OLIVETTI

Like — did she have any close friends she might confide in — things she wouldn't even tell you? Did she keep letters, a journal,

a diary?
>	(DIANE hesitates.)
What?

                    DIANE
No, nothing.

                    OLIVETTI
Those kinds of things.
>	(DIANE does not respond.)
It's just a theory. If you think of anything —

                    DIANE
I'll let you know.

                    OLIVETTI
Thank you.
>	(A beat.)
I hope you'll keep what I've told you in confidence. For your own
sake, if for no other reason.

                    DIANE
>	(Sarcastically.)
Afraid Tom will try to silence me, too?

                    OLIVETTI
I think it would be best if he didn't know we'd spoken.
>	(Looks at his watch.)
Well, I have to go re-interview Mark Lowery. If he's smart, he
won't talk to me. Which won't leave us with much, regardless of
what the jury found. It's awfully hard to re-try a different person
for the same crime. The son-of-a-bitch might just get away with it.

>	(OLIVETTI goes off right. After making sure he is gone,
>	DIANE goes to the closed suitcase, sets it down, opens it, and
>	rummages around until she finds the DIARY. It is held
>	closed with a locked strap that DIANE tries to unlock, but
>	cannot.

>	Meanwhile, OLIVETTI appears in a spotlight at the right of
>	the FRONT AREA holding the DIARY. He reads aloud.)

OLIVETTI

How can I keep doing this to my own sister?   And in her own house.   Each night, he waits for her sedatives to take, and comes to my room.   In the morning, I feel so guilty I want to hide under the covers.   But I can't refuse him.   What's wrong with me?   I never wanted him this way.   He's got to tell her.

> (*While OLIVETTI is reading, DIANE exits momentary and returns with a chrome letter opener.   She tries to pry the DI-ARY open with the letter opener.   Finally, she succeeds, breaking the clasp.   She flips through the pages, stops, flips again, until she finds something and reads it to herself.   She starts to break down.*)

OLIVETTI
(*Reading aloud continuously.*)
I've told him that over and over.   He makes promises, then excuses.   If he doesn't, I will.   I've told him that, too.   Any day now —

> (*The DIARY falls from DIANE's hand.   As the light fades on OLIVETTI, DIANE contemplates the letter opener she still holds in her other hand.*)

DIANE
Or maybe the sons-of-bitches *won't* get away with it.

> (*The lights fade on DIANE and come up on OLIVETTI and LOWERY, in another part of the FRONT AREA.*)

LOWERY
Talk to my lawyer.

OLIVETTI
And who might that be?

LOWERY
Thomas Russo.

OLIVETTI
Is that a fact?   After the things he said about you.

LOWERY

He didn't believe them. He was only doing his job.

OLIVETTI

You might be right about that.

LOWERY

He told me so. He knows no one framed Jennifer.

OLIVETTI

Does he now?

(The lights fade on the FRONT AREA and come up on RUS-SO's office as RUSSO enters.)

VOICE of SECRETARY

(On the intercom.)

Mr. Russo?

(RUSSO hits speaker button on his phone.)

RUSSO

Yes, Stephanie.

VOICE of SECRETARY

Your mail is on your desk, Mr. Russo. There was also a telephone message from Mark Lowery's secretary. Dr. Lowery would like you to come to his home as soon as you can. He says it's an emergency. The address is on the message.

RUSSO

Okay — and I know the address.

(A spotlight comes up on the FRONT AREA. LOWERY is lying dead on the floor, with a gold-plated letter opener in his chest.

RUSSO checks around his desk while picking up his letters.)

RUSSO

Stephanie, did you see my letter opener?

(He continues looking as the lights on RUSSO fade.)

VOICE of FIRST TV REPORTER

For the third time this year, murder has descended on this upscale community.   Dr. Mark Lowery, forty-one, was found fatally stabbed in the chest earlier today in his home.

(During this, OLIVETTI, his hands in surgical gloves, cross-es to LOWERY's body, kneels, removes the letter opener, ex-amines it, and glances in the general direction of RUSSO's desk.)

VOICE of SECOND TV REPORTER
(Overlapping.)

Lowery was the husband of thirty-six-year-old Christine Lowery, herself murdered just months ago at the same residence.   Police believe the two crimes are connected.

(The lights fade.)

VOICE of THIRD TV REPORTER
(Overlapping.)

Police are also investigating a possible connection between Dr. Lowery's murder and the bludgeoning death of forty-year-old He-len Jamieson last month.   Search warrants have been issued for both crime scenes.

(A spotlight catches OLIVETTI in the FRONT AREA hold-ing the DIARY very carefully in his gloved hands. He briefly examines its distinctive design, loose strap, and broken clasp, as the lights fade.)

CURTAIN

END OF PLAY

AT LONG LAST, A NEW STAGE THRILLER

by Richard Weill

[*Mr. Weill is the author of* Framed, *a new stage thriller premiering May 7 at the Elite Theatre (South Stage) in Oxnard.* Framed *is directed by Judy Blake.*]

The current health of the stage thriller quite resembles a scene common to several of the genre's most famous plays. Before our very eyes, the thriller is shot, stabbed, strangled, and officially pronounced dead by persons of unimpeachable credibility. The thriller audience is left shaken and horrified as the curtain rings down. But as the thriller faithful well know, all is not always as it appears. What was once pronounced dead in Act I could still reappear in Act II, as full of life as ever. Couldn't it?

Shortly before his death in 2001, *Sleuth* author Anthony Shaffer lamented that he was "just in time to drink about the last of the *Sleuth* vintage wine … I don't think there's that much of it left." Sadly, too often he's been proven correct. Although plays like *Sleuth, Deathtrap, Dial 'M' for Murder, Wait Until Dark, Angel Street, Ten Little Indians, Witness for the Prosecution* continue to attract large audiences across the country and around the world, new successful stage thrillers are few and far between.

Why is that? The longest-running play or musical in theater history is a thriller (Agatha Christie's *The Mousetrap*, running continuously in London's West End since 1952). The longest-running play in Broadway or off-Broadway history is also a thriller (Warren Manzi's *Perfect Crime*, still running off-Broadway since 1987). Why is a genre that remains so popular now so rare?

Indeed, Shaffer believed that "you can astound more in the playhouse than in the movie house." In movies, "you can do everything," so "the audience tends to believe less and less, and you will increasingly find that you can actually achieve less and less." That isn't true with a stage play. Shaffer also believed "that under the guise of the thriller form you can deliver a message without seeming to do so, without boring people."

After all, who doesn't enjoy sitting in a theater, engrossed in a story, when as intermission approaches — BAM! — something happens to change the meaning of everything you've seen since the curtain rose? Not with special effects or trick photography. Only with good storytelling: a handful of characters — listed for you in a theater program, no less — often on a single set. No room for frills, but just enough room for surprises.

And then, after you've spent the intermission debating who saw the Act I twist coming — WHAM! — Act II brings another twist that shifts the meaning of everything once again. Who doesn't enjoy such a roller-coaster ride — one hopefully finishing with an ironic ending that is both astonishing and inevitable? Very few, I suspect.

The simple answer to why more stage thrillers aren't written is that they're damn hard to write! *Deathtrap* author Ira Levin called the stage thriller "that trickiest and most demanding of genres." Particularly in the era of movies and television, said Levin, a thriller play "has to have something special, something that will work on stage." John Pielmeier, whose 1999 play *Voices in the Dark* won the Edgar Allan Poe Award as Best Mystery Play, likewise considers the thriller "absolutely the most challenging form to write for the theatre."

To be sure, no other genre places as high a premium on originality. As Levin wrote in *Deathtrap* itself, "every possible variation seems to have been played"; the author is tested to "conjure up a few new ones."

But not just any new twist will do; each twist also must be fair. Producer Lawrence Langner phrased it this way: "It is permissible to deceive the audience under conditions where the characters in the play are also deceived in the same way, so that the situation is unraveled for all of us together. However, it usually spells disaster if the characters on stage know the real situation or truth, but the author deliberately sets out to deceive us."

Then again, a thriller cannot only be about shocks and twists. Agatha Christie, author of such classic stage thrillers as *Witness for the Prosecution, Ten Little Indians*, and *The Mousetrap*, warned: "It is a limitation to have to rely entirely on your thrills or surprises."

Rather, "the more firmly you place your plot in everyday sur-
roundings, and have characters with a life of their own, the more
effective your drama will be."

Theater critic Jack Kroll once called it all "the inexorable, interlocking inevitability of the ultimate thriller." Are you beginning to
see the difficulty?

My play *Framed* originated with an idea I first had in 1992. I
didn't think of the second twist until 2008, when I started finally
to map out the details of the play. In fact, my map was so detailed
that I wrote the first draft over a single weekend — everything
except the ending, which didn't occur to me until weeks later. After four drafts, I submitted it to a competition. It didn't win. Several major rewrites followed. After eight drafts, the play was giv-
en a reading before an audience at the William Esper Studio in
Manhattan in 2013. That led to drafts nine and ten. See what I
mean?

Tom Eubanks, artistic director of the Elite Theatre in Oxnard, contacted me in 2014 after reading my play. He said he was interested in producing it, but couldn't fit it into the 2015 season. He
asked if I would wait another year. I agreed. A year later, he
called again. Judy Blake signed on to direct. *Framed* was about to
become a reality.

Framed is about two lawyers defending a rich young woman
charged with murder. A virtual mountain of forensic evidence
proves her guilt: blood evidence, fiber evidence, gunshot residue,
cellphone records, and ultimately ballistic evidence. The older of
the two experienced lawyers, refusing to gamble with the life of
his client, declares the case unwinnable. He wants to make a plea
deal with the prosecutor. But his younger, slicker, and more famous colleague — who's also an audacious media hound — will
entertain no thoughts of defeat. Great legal careers require stun-
ning victories. If a mountain of evidence exists, it can only mean
that a mountain of evidence was deliberately planted to incrimi-
nate the rich young defendant. In short, she must have been
framed!

Actually, the play's title has a double meaning. In an early scene,
we learn that the celebrity half of the legal team decorates his of-

fice, his waiting room, even his men's room with framed articles and photographs marking the highlights of his career.   So "framed" not only is his defense strategy; it also symbolizes that, unlike his less flamboyant, more risk-averse co-counsel, this lawyer is driven by his ego.   Has his judgment been clouded by the image of invincibility he's long created for himself?

That's about all I'm at liberty to say.   With a thriller, you must hook your audience using as little bait as possible.   Spoil the surprises, spoil the play.

Hopefully, what I've written here is enough to make you bite.   If it is, come to the South Stage of the Elite Theatre in Oxnard on May 7-8, 14-15, or 21-22 to find out the whole story.   Maybe the late Anthony Shaffer was wrong after all.   Maybe just enough of the "*Sleuth* vintage wine" is still in the bottle.

Intrigue abounds in *Framed* at the Elite

by Jim Spencer and Shirley Lorraine

Now through May 22 Oxnard's Elite Theatre Company it is presenting a world premiere murder mystery thriller entitled *Framed*.

The story has multiple murders, multiple lawyers, multiple potential culprits, and possibly multiple frame-ups. It is full of twists and turns. One moment the identity of a guilty party appears clear, and the next the same party seems in the clear. The script is engaging, entertaining, highly credible, and well worth your time.

First, there's a murder. Voice over clips of TV news reports about the crime effectively set up the plot and move the audience right into the action.

The accused's seasoned attorney, Eugene Murray (Larry Swartz), confers with a colleague, Thomas Russo (Alexander Schottky), about possible strategies in defending the case as all the evidence points to the guilt of his client, played by Olivia Heulitt. New circumstances begin to emerge to suggest the defendant may have been framed after Russo, who is known for his outlandish and headline-hunting tactics, joins the case.

But that's only the beginning. A subsequent murder and other complications send the story cascading in various directions — leaving the audience and detective Olivetti (Ken Johnson) the job of deductively connecting the dots to see if they form a frame.

The play's author, Richard Weill, is both a trial attorney and an experienced playwright. Consequently, the script bears an uncommon authenticity, as well as being literate, concise and cogent. His characters offer valuable insights on the differences between being "innocent" and "not guilty," plus richly balanced observations about the impact of the media on the justice system.

The characters spend a lot of time talking about legal issues, which makes the play predictably wordy. To counterbalance the wordiness, director Judy Blake appropriately keeps the tempo fast paced. Each act was only 45 minutes long. But this positive technique has a slight downside. The verbal action is often so rapid that major points can easily be missed. There isn't time to savor the intellectual morsels playwright Weill shares through his characters.

All new works benefit from fine tuning. In this play there is a surprise ending. It is presented abruptly, almost without warning, and then the curtain falls. Boom! The show is over. In our view the audience is not given enough time to fully take in what happened before the house lights come up. Some type of short closing epilogue scene could wrap up the storyline.

By their nature, mystery thrillers are roller coaster rides. Good ones require top notch casts to make the experience real for the audience. Lead by Alexander Schottky as brash defense attorney Thomas Russo, the ensemble at the Elite is more than up to the job. It does a marvelous job of engaging and transporting the audience through all the twists and loops on the search to find out who did it and who, if anyone, was framed.

Whodunit 'Framed' will keep audience guessing

New play makes debut at Elite Theatre

By Rita Moran
Arts Critic

It's not often a local theater company presents the premiere of a new work, and even less frequently that play is by a New York attorney and former prosecutor.

REVIEW

Oxnard's Elite Theatre Company has distinguished itself in seeking out original plays that allow authors to see their creations staged in a small theater with talented, local actors and audiences eager to experience fresh creations. Behind the troupe's wide-ranging productions, which include an annual new short-play competition, is artistic director Tom Eubanks. Based in the Channel Islands area, Elite boasts two stages, its larger main stage and the more intimate South Stage, where Richard Weill's "Framed" is now playing.

Weill's courtroom experience is evident in both the attorneys' background discussions and in the snippets of trial scenes in a play that opens with a dead body — and it's not the last of them.

There are of course the usual suspects, most specifically the young defendant, Jennifer Creighton (Olivia Heulitt). She seems to be a suspect when a woman is killed and Creighton is found with the victim's blood spattered on her along with other incriminating details. Heulitt is called upon to be secretive at first, then more concerned as evidence stacks up against her.

Creighton's methodic defense attorney, Eugene Murphy (Larry Swartz), is sensibly cautious, but when he consults with the slicker Thomas Russo (Alexander Schottky), he finds Russo is not shy about bending the facts or shading the truth.

Russo's expansive office is the main set for the play, which unfolds in snippets keyed by detective George Olivetti (Ken Johnson) as he pages through a diary related to the case. Johnson, who reads elegantly between each "live" scene, is also involved with other characters as he whips between his solo discoveries in the diary, spotlighted at the edge of the stage, then periodically makes it onto the central playing field to interact with the attorneys.

It turns out that Russo has a wife, Diane (Nancy Solomons), who makes too many bothersome phone calls to her husband's office, as far as he's concerned, while seemingly too insecure or ill to leave her house. Her calls interrupt while he is urging Murphy to employ a less straightforward investigation and defense for Creighton. Solomons delivers a reversal of character later when she shows up in Russo's office neat and sharp-witted.

Part of the intrigue involves around a dinner date arranged on the night of the murder between Creighton and her somewhat secret boyfriend, Mark Lowery (played with low-key smoothness by Johnny Avila). The woman whose murder kicks off the tale was Lowery's wife.

Possibly the only "clean" characters are Johnson's Olivetti, Swartz's Murphy and the prosecutor, played with convincing realism by Jake Mailey.

The playwright scatters lots of distracting facts, discoveries and oddities throughout the script, which occasionally feels like Agatha Christie and the suspicious collection of characters in her mysteries.

The result can be confusing, as obviously intended, but also amusing as the basic battle plays out between the honest gumshoe approach and the truth-fudging but financially successful ways of Russo.

Judy Blake directs the fast-paced play with its flashes of action, confrontation and ambiguity.

About the Author

Richard Weill, a practicing lawyer and former prosecutor in Westchester County, New York, has been writing plays since 1976. In 2016, his legal thriller *Framed* premiered in Oxnard, California to critical acclaim, standing-room-only audiences, and a run extended by popular demand. His play *Sisters*, suggested by an unsolved 1966 murder, starts in the present and moves backwards scene-by-scene to tell the story of how a crime changed a prominent family — and why.

Besides *Sisters* and *Framed*, Mr. Weill has written a fictional version of Agatha Christie's 1926 disappearance (*Imperfect Alibi*), a comedy-drama set in 1950's New York about the 23-year collaboration of two mystery writers (*Hardbound*); a thriller about adultery and betrayal (*The Other Woman*), a two-character thriller (*Seed of Doubt*), and an evening of three short plays about crime and crime writers (*Constant Companions*).

In addition, Mr. Weill has written two plays about young artists (*Emergence of the Soul*; *The Unframed Canvas*), a political comedy (*Another County Heard From*), a one-man play (*This ... Is Murrow*), an allegory about baseball's Black Sox scandal (*And the Echo Answered Fraud*), a play set in the New York Civil Jail (*This Little World*), a musical version of Waiting for Godot (*The Vaudevillians*), and a screenplay about a baseball broadcaster (*The Voice of Summer*).

He is a member of the Dramatists Guild.

Made in the USA
Las Vegas, NV
23 October 2021

32947914R10100